Joined by Fate:
INTERTWINED BIOGRAPHIES

ABRAHAM LINCOLN

AND

JOHN WILKES BOOTH

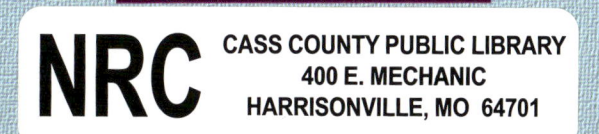

Joined by Fate:
INTERTWINED BIOGRAPHIES

ABRAHAM LINCOLN
AND
JOHN WILKES BOOTH

DONNA M. BOZZONE, PhD

Enslow Publishing
101 W. 23rd Street
Suite 240
New York, NY 10011
USA

enslow.com

Published in 2019 by Enslow Publishing, LLC.
101 W. 23rd Street, Suite 240, New York, NY 10011

Copyright © 2019 by Enslow Publishing, LLC.

All rights reserved.

No part of this book may be reproduced by any means without the written permission of the publisher.

Library of Congress Cataloging-in-Publication Data

Names: Bozzone, Donna M., author.
Title: Abraham Lincoln and John Wilkes Booth / Donna M. Bozzone, PhD.
Description: New York : Enslow, 2019. | Series: Joined by Fate : intertwined biographies | Includes bibliographical references and index. | Audience: Grades 7 to 12.
Identifiers: LCCN 2017055267| ISBN 9780766098091 (library bound) | ISBN 9780766098107 (pbk.)
Subjects: LCSH: Lincoln, Abraham, 1809–1865—Assassination. | Lincoln, Abraham, 1809–1865. | Booth, John Wilkes, 1838–1865. | Presidents—United States—Biography. | Assassins—United States—Biography.
Classification: LCC E457.5 .B79 2018 | DDC 973.7092/2—dc23
LC record available at https://lccn.loc.gov/2017055267

Printed in the United States of America

To Our Readers: We have done our best to make sure all website addresses in this book were active and appropriate when we went to press. However, the author and the publisher have no control over and assume no liability for the material available on those websites or on any websites they may link to. Any comments or suggestions can be sent by e-mail to customerservice@enslow.com.

Photo Credits: Cover, p. 3 (left), p. 97 Everett Historical/Shutterstock.com; cover, p. 3 (right), pp. 6, 12, 34, 40, 46, 57, 61, 65, 67, 70–71, 75, 80, 82, 87, 104–105 Library of Congress Prints and Photographs Division; pp. 19, 26 Corbis Historical/Getty Images; pp. 23, 94–95 Bettmann/Getty Images; p. 29 MPI/Archive Photos/Getty Images; p. 30 Pictorial Press Ltd/Alamy Stock Photo; p. 37 Classic Image/Alamy Stock Photo; p. 50 Universal History Archive/Universal Images Group/Getty Images; p. 54 GraphicaArtis/Archive Photos/Getty Images; p. 90 © North Wind Picture Archives; p. 99 State Archives of Florida/Florida Memory/Alamy Stock Photo; p. 109 Buyenlarge/Archive Photos/Getty Images; pp. 110–111 Masaki Norton/Shutterstock.com.

CONTENTS

	Introduction	7
CHAPTER 1	Lincoln's Boyhood	9
CHAPTER 2	Booth's Early Years	22
CHAPTER 3	New Salem and the Presidency	32
CHAPTER 4	Politics and Acting	48
CHAPTER 5	The Presidential Election	58
CHAPTER 6	The Civil War	73
CHAPTER 7	The Assassination	86
CHAPTER 8	Lincoln's and Booth's Legacies	98
	Chronology	113
	Chapter Notes	119
	Glossary	123
	Further Reading	125
	Index	126

The War Department distributed a wanted poster for Booth after he assassinated President Lincoln. The reward of $100,000 is worth roughly $1.62 million in today's money.

INTRODUCTION

General Robert E. Lee surrendered his army on April 9, 1865, a move that ended the US Civil War. This conflict, which pitted American against American, had raged for almost four years to the day. The Civil War was by far the deadliest military event in United States history, with more than 620,000 casualties. In fact, more Americans died in the Civil War than died in both world wars, the Korean War, and the Vietnam War combined.

The loss of a loved one in the Civil War touched almost every family. In 1860, the US population was approximately 31 million. Today, it is about 326 million. If the same proportion of Americans died now as did during the Civil War, it would mean a loss of six million lives. Moreover, the Civil War took place in a much smaller United States than exists today. In the 1860s, just thirty-three states made up the country, compared to fifty today. And the war did not spread to each state but to only twenty-three.

Abraham Lincoln served as US president during the Civil War. Lincoln's election led to the secession of the Southern states that formed the Confederacy. Lincoln oversaw the Union's war effort and restored the country. He never recognized the Confederate States of America as an independent nation and wanted all states to reunite and forge a peace with "malice toward none; with charity for all."[1]

ABRAHAM LINCOLN and JOHN WILKES BOOTH

On April 11, 1865, President Lincoln stepped out on a balcony on the White House to address a crowd that had gathered to hear him speak about the Confederacy's surrender. One part of Lincoln's speech broke new ground. He said, "I would myself prefer it [the right to vote] were conferred on the very intelligent [literate blacks] and on those who served our cause as soldiers."[2] Lincoln was proposing that at least some of the newly emancipated slaves would have the right to vote.

A man named John Wilkes Booth watched Lincoln that night from the crowd. A popular actor from a family full of actors, Booth was a Confederate sympathizer. Unlike many others gathered, Booth did not like the idea of citizenship and its privileges for blacks. He turned to his friends and said, "...by God, I'll put him through. That is the last speech he will ever make."[3] He concluded that "our cause being lost, something decisive must be done."[4] Booth hated Lincoln with a single-minded intensity and blamed him for the loss of the Confederacy.

Lincoln and Booth were each heading toward calamity. On April 14, 1865, Lincoln attended the theater to see a performance of the play *Our American Cousin*. Booth entered the theater box where Lincoln sat and shot him in the head. Lincoln died early the next morning.

What goals, accomplishments, dreams, and life journeys did each of these men have, and how did fate unite them in this terrible way? To understand this story, we need to explore their lives and the world they inhabited—America in the nineteenth century.

Chapter 1

LINCOLN'S BOYHOOD

In 1859, when Abraham Lincoln was trying to win the Republican Party's presidential nomination, *Chicago Tribune* reporter John Locke Scripps asked him for some information about his background. Lincoln had little to offer him, though. "Why Scripps," he replied, "… it is a great piece of folly to attempt to make anything out of my early life. It can all be condensed into a single sentence … The short and simple annals of the poor. That's my life, and that's all you or anyone else can make of it."[1]

It is true that Abraham Lincoln was born and raised in difficult circumstances. He had to work hard, physically, from the time he was a little boy. Sometimes he went to bed hungry. Yet his ancestors were actually financially well off, as were some of his living relatives. So, what happened to Lincoln's branch of the family that theirs was a life of struggle?

Abraham Lincoln's Origins

Lincoln's paternal relatives came from England, but less is known about his mother's ancestry. In 1637, Samuel Lincoln moved to Hingham, Massachusetts. A weaver in England, Samuel became a successful trader and businessman in America. Mordecai, one of Samuel's grandsons, achieved even more success. He was a wealthy landowner in Pennsylvania and part of the economic and social elite of his time. Mordecai's son John sought and found his fortune in Virginia's Shenandoah Valley, where he established a large farm. Captain Abraham, John Lincoln's son, got his start thanks to a gift of two hundred acres of Virginia farmland from his grandfather Mordecai. Captain Abraham Lincoln had three sons: Mordecai, Josiah, and Thomas. Thomas would father the future President Lincoln. The Lincoln family was doing well, improving their circumstances with each generation.

All of that changed in a day. A terrible day.

Daniel Boone, Frontiersman

Born in 1734, Daniel Boone was an accomplished hunter and woodsman. He is most famous for exploring and settling Kentucky. Boone blazed a trail to the western frontier through the Cumberland Gap and established the first American settlement west of the Appalachian Mountains. Before the end of the eighteenth century, more than 200,000 people followed his route into Kentucky to start new lives. President Lincoln's grandfather Captain Abraham Lincoln and his family were part of that population of 200,000 who moved to Kentucky because of Boone's recommendation.

A folk hero in his time and in literature and popular culture today, Boone has been the subject of stories and books. For example, author James Fennimore Cooper based the main character in the *Leatherstocking Tales* on him. Boone has also been depicted in movies and in a television series from 1964 to 1970. He has even appeared on postage stamps.

LINCOLN'S BOYHOOD

Captain Abraham Lincoln sold his farm in Virginia and moved to Kentucky, having heard that opportunity was plentiful there. He was quite successful, amassing more than 5,500 acres of rich farmland. One day, Captain Abraham and his three sons were planting corn when American Indians attacked them. Captain Abraham was killed instantly. His fifteen-year-old son, Mordecai, sent his younger brother Josiah for help. The youngest brother, Thomas, was only eight years old. He saw his father murdered, and as the little boy sat next to the body, Mordecai saw that another Native American was about to hurt Thomas. Mordecai aimed his rifle and shot the attacker dead. Thomas witnessed this too.

Due to the laws of inheritance in Kentucky then, the oldest son inherited the entire estate—everything. So, Mordecai acquired his father's wealth and led a financially stable life. But Josiah and Thomas had to make their own way.

Instead of living as the heir of a well-to-do Kentucky farmer, Thomas had to work to earn his keep. Completely uneducated, Thomas worked as hard as he could and was as successful as possible, given his circumstances.

Thomas Lincoln married Nancy Hanks in 1806. Their first child, Sarah, was born eight months later. He bought three hundred acres of land along Nolan Creek in Kentucky. Thomas called his home Sinking Spring Farm and built a small log cabin (fewer than three hundred square feet). The cabin consisted of one room; it had a dirt floor and no glass windows. Although modest, this cabin was as large as about 90 percent of pioneer cabins in the area. There,

After his father's murder, Thomas, the youngest son in the family, inherited nothing because of the inheritance laws of the time.

ABRAHAM LINCOLN and JOHN WILKES BOOTH

Thomas Lincoln, shown here later in life, was born in 1778. When he died in 1851, Abraham Lincoln did not attend his father's funeral.

LINCOLN'S BOYHOOD

Nancy Hanks gave birth to Abraham Lincoln on February 12, 1809, but the Lincolns moved away from Sinking Spring before Abraham was two years old.

They moved about ten miles (16 km) away to a smaller but more fertile property by Knob Creek. In 1812, Thomas and Nancy had another son. They named the boy Thomas after his father. Sadly, the child died in infancy.

The move from Sinking Spring to Knob Creek marked the first of many Lincoln family relocations. In 1816, the Lincolns left Kentucky, crossing the Ohio River, to make a life in Indiana. As Abraham described many years later, his father left Kentucky "partly on account of slavery, but chiefly on account of the difficulty in land titles in Ky."[2] Thomas Lincoln opposed slavery for religious reasons, as he and his wife belonged to a church that forbade this shameful, immoral practice. He also had economic reasons for opposing slavery.

Kentucky entered the Union as a slave state in 1792. Farmers like Thomas Lincoln could not compete with farms powered by slave labor. Also, Kentucky had no reliable system for surveying land, so getting a clear title to property proved difficult. Thomas had purchased three parcels of Kentucky farmland and could not get legal proof of his ownership. He found Indiana, mostly still wilderness, attractive because of its ban on slavery. In addition, the federal government surveyed the land and provided clear titles of ownership.

So in the fall of 1816, Thomas Lincoln traveled to Indiana by himself to find a place to stake a land claim to homestead. He chose Pigeon Creek, a forested, almost completely unoccupied area. He built a three-sided camp, marked the corners of the land he claimed with piles of branches and leaves, and returned to Kentucky for his family.

The journey from Kentucky to Indiana was an arduous one. The Lincolns had to hack their way through vegetation,

ABRAHAM LINCOLN and JOHN WILKES BOOTH

Lincoln lived in small log cabins throughout his childhood in each of the places his family homesteaded. Here is the log cabin Lincoln and his father built in Illinois in 1831.

and wild animals such as bears, wolves, and bobcats roamed the wilderness. The entire trip was more than one hundred miles. Once the Lincolns arrived, they camped for a few days. They lit a fire and wrapped up in animal skins to keep warm. Thomas later built a log cabin.

The Lincolns' first year was hard. They managed to survive the winter by eating deer and bear meat. Abraham, still a little boy, once shot a turkey for the family's dinner. Killing an animal upset him so much that he never did it again. Once winter passed, the Lincolns had to clear the land for farming. Strong for an eight year old, Abraham swung an axe to cut down trees.

LINCOLN'S BOYHOOD

As time went by, the Lincoln family seemed to be settling nicely. Nancy certainly felt more at home once her aunt and uncle, Elizabeth and Thomas Sparrow, moved to Pigeon Creek along with their nephew, Dennis Hanks. Life was going well.

All of this changed dramatically. First, a horse kicked Abraham in the head. The blow was so powerful that witnesses thought Abraham was dead. They summoned his father, and Abraham regained consciousness. Hours passed before he could speak again, however.

After the episode with the horse came milk sickness, a disease caused by drinking the milk of cows that consume white snakeroot plants. Chemicals from the plants seep into the cow milk, making it poisonous. Tragically, the Sparrows died.

Next, Abrahams's mother, Nancy, became ill with milk sickness. She died at age thirty-four. Abraham was not yet ten.

With her mother gone, twelve-year-old Sarah Lincoln tried her best to cook, clean, and keep house. Sometimes, she could not bear having lost Nancy and sat by the fire and cried. Thomas Lincoln and Dennis Hanks hunted to provide food. Abraham tried to comfort his sister, but he also resented his father for making him do hard labor. He and his father grew increasingly distant.

A New Family and New Life

Thomas Lincoln went back to Kentucky and married a friend, Sarah (Sally) Bush Johnston, a widow with three children. Sally transformed Abraham's life. When she arrived at the Lincoln home in Indiana, she saw dirty, poorly clothed, and hungry children. She scrubbed them and the cabin clean. Sally made a home for them all. At her urging, Thomas improved the cabin by building a wood floor to cover the dirt one, a finished roof that did not leak, a window, and a functional door. She also had him make a loft where the boys could sleep. Most importantly, Sally

ABRAHAM LINCOLN and JOHN WILKES BOOTH

Sarah Lincoln was Abraham Lincoln's stepmother. She was born in 1788 and died in 1869. She lived long enough to see her fears realized, namely the murder of her beloved stepson.

LINCOLN'S BOYHOOD

brought love. Abraham loved her and later remembered that the years in Indiana were happy once his stepmother arrived.

Despite the improved care Sally gave the family, life remained challenging for Abraham. He had to work so hard that he had few chances to go to school. He only attended classes for a few days, weeks, or months at a time. Abraham likely did not receive more than a year of school in total.

However, Abraham loved to read and was a lifelong learner. One of his relatives recalled that when Abraham finished his work, he would come home and "go to the cupboard, snatch a piece of corn bread, take down a book, sit down in a chair, cock his legs up as high as his head, and read."[3] Abraham preferred reading to frontier life, where he not only worked for his family but for others, at his father's request. Despite his labor, people sometimes called him lazy because he was "reading, scribbling, writing, ciphering, writing Poetry, etc."[4]

It was not easy to find books to read in the wilderness. Abraham's neighbors recalled how he would walk miles to borrow a book. He probably read and reread his family's Bible and several other books popular at the time: *Aesop's Fables*, *Pilgrims Progress*, *Robinson Crusoe*, the *Arabian Nights*, *The Life of Washington*, and Benjamin Franklin's autobiography. Abraham memorized many passages from these books.

As Abraham grew from a child into a teenager, he shot up in height, reaching 6 feet 2 inches (188 centimeters) by age sixteen. Weighing only 160 pounds (72.5 kilograms), he was lean and lanky. Yet, he turned out to be a fast runner and strong wrestler. Also an excellent speller and writer, his illiterate neighbors often asked him to write letters for them. While sometimes sad and shy, Abraham could also be lively and enchant people with jokes and funny stories.

As Abraham got older, Thomas relied on him more for work and hired him out more. Some people observed that Thomas appeared to favor his stepson, John Johnston, over Abraham. According to the law then, until he was twenty-one years old, Abraham had to hand over all of his earnings to his father. He yearned for adventure and some type of work besides farming, felling trees, and splitting rails to make fences.

Over the course of his life, Abraham never said a positive word about his father. When his sister Sarah and stepsister Matilda both married and moved out of the Lincoln home, Abraham felt even more alienated.

He got a job working in a ferryboat business on the Ohio River. He also picked up additional jobs plowing fields and building fences. He managed to make around six dollars a month. He built a flatboat of his own and, to his amazement, earned a dollar by taking two men out to a steamship coming down the river.

Unfortunately, life delivered another punch to the Lincoln family; Abraham's sister Sarah died giving birth to her first child, a stillborn baby. Three months later, in April 1828, a grieving Abraham left home again when he was hired to take a flatboat with produce and supplies to New Orleans, Louisiana.

The 1,200-mile (1,931-kilometer) journey to New Orleans, down the Ohio and Mississippi rivers, was a dangerous one. Abraham, only nineteen, and Allen Gentry, the boat owner's son, faced changing currents, sandbars, and thick, tangled vegetation along the riverbanks. In addition to these hazards, a group of eight men attacked the pair in Baton Rouge, Louisiana. The group tried to steal their

Seeing slaves chained and mistreated affected Lincoln deeply. It was the first time he witnessed the horror of human slavery.

LINCOLN'S BOYHOOD

Here is an artist's version of a young Abraham Lincoln as he may have looked on his flatboat during his early days as a river pilot.

ABRAHAM LINCOLN and JOHN WILKES BOOTH

cargo. Somehow, Abraham and Allen managed to save their goods and escape serious harm. They arrived in New Orleans, the biggest and most populous city Abraham had ever seen. There, he saw a slave market for the first time.

Having delivered the goods he had transported to New Orleans, Abraham sold the flatboat and returned home. Once again, he gave his full earnings to his father.

In 1836, Thomas Lincoln moved the family again—this time to Illinois, a non-slave-holding state. The reason for this move is not entirely clear. Thomas may have been worried about another outbreak of milk sickness.

Abraham helped his family make the 200-mile (322-km) trek to their new home. He helped clear the land, plant crops, split rails, make fences, and build a cabin. Once the family settled in Illinois, Abraham couldn't wait to make a life for himself.

The Nation's Highways: Rivers

During the nineteenth century, the US labor force largely worked on farms. Roads were rough, poorly maintained, or nonexistent in most places, and water was the only way for farmers to get their produce to market. As a result, people settled along waterways, such as rivers, and eventually developed canals.

Farmers in the US interior could send goods throughout the country by flatboats, such as the ones Lincoln piloted, or steamboats that permitted travel upstream against strong currents. The commerce "water highways" made it possible for cities such as New Orleans, St. Louis, Cincinnati, and New York to thrive.

LINCOLN'S BOYHOOD

Old enough to go out on his own, Abraham, his cousin John Hanks, and his stepbrother John Johnston built a flatboat. A man named Denton Offutt hired them to transport a load of goods to New Orleans. They headed out in April 1831, starting on the Sangamon River in Illinois, on to the Illinois River, and then the Mississippi. The trip almost ended before it started, as the Sangamon River was so low the boat got stuck in New Salem, Illinois. It soon began to take on water. Abraham managed to prevent disaster. He unloaded some of the cargo onto the riverbank, borrowed a hand drill to make a hole to let out the water, repaired the hole, and off they went.

Offutt joined Abraham and the other young men for the journey. He found Abraham and New Salem, the town where they temporarily got stuck, impressive. He told Abraham he planned to open a general store in New Salem and asked him to run it.

After New Orleans, Abraham returned to New Salem. Unfortunately, Offutt proved to be all talk; there was no store. But Abraham had also liked New Salem. He decided to stay in an effort to start his adult life away from the frontier. He remained in New Salem for the next six years.

Chapter 2

BOOTH'S EARLY YEARS

John Wilkes Booth had his fortune read when he was twelve years old. The fortuneteller told John that he was born under an unlucky star and would die young. She said he would have a fast, short, but grand life. "Young sir, I've never seen a worse hand. I wish I hadn't seen it."[1] John wrote down the prophecy and kept it with him. He unfolded the paper to look at it so much that it became worn.

Although John felt unlucky, he had a definite ambition, which he revealed to his sister Asia. "I must have fame! fame!"[2] he told her. And John did achieve fame as a stage actor in his time. He also achieved infamy as the man who killed Abraham Lincoln. How did his life lead to this terrible event? Unfortunately, there's no definite answer to this question, but examining his life from the outset offers some clues.

Booth's Origins

John's ancestors were from England. His father, Junius Brutus Booth, emigrated from the country in 1821. He was a well-regarded actor, and John's mother, Mary Ann, was a seed merchant's daughter. Junius and Mary Ann met one evening when she was selling flowers outside the theater where he

BOOTH'S EARLY YEARS

Junius Brutus Booth was born in 1796. He moved to the United States in 1821 and became one of the best actors of his generation.

performed. After a brief courtship, they married in January 1821 and sailed to the United States a few weeks later.

Junius had performed many places in the United States but chose to make Maryland his home. He leased 150 acres just outside of Bel Air village. They lived not too far from Baltimore, then the nation's second largest city. Junius had a two-story log home built and began transforming the property into a farm. Over time, he built a dairy and a barn with stables, put in a pond, and planted fruit trees. A native of London, Mary Ann did not enjoy the "pioneer-like" life her husband was fashioning. Fortunately, their neighbor Elizabeth taught Mary how to bake bread and other household and outdoor basics.

While Junius and Mary Ann weren't great farmers, they excelled at expanding their family. Beginning in 1821, they had a new baby approximately every two years: Junius Jr. (called June by the family, 1821), Rosalie (1823), Henry (1825), Mary Ann (1827), Frederick (1829), Elizabeth (1831), Edwin (1833), Asia (1835), John (1838), and Joseph (1840). Only six of these children reached adulthood. Henry, Mary Ann, Frederick, and Elizabeth all died before John was born.

Junius was drunk at a local tavern when John arrived. Their neighbor Elizabeth, also known as Aunty Rogers, helped to deliver him. Openly his parents' favorite, John was named after John Wilkes, the eighteenth-century radical. Wilkes opposed tyranny and the king; he fought for the rights of the common people. John Wilkes Booth took pride in his name, declaring, "It meant liberty."[3]

Junius was a troubled man. When performing at theaters across the country, Junius sometimes had violent outbursts. By the time John was born, his father had shot a man, assaulted others, attempted suicide three times, and been jailed in four states. He also wrote a letter to President Andrew Jackson, threatening to slit his throat. He wandered naked in a snowstorm, tried to

BOOTH'S EARLY YEARS

kill a sleeping friend, and offered to sell his son Edwin for $5. Alcohol contributed to many of these events. Junius was calmer on the farm, where he kept no liquor.

Junius's father, Richard, emigrated from England in 1823 to join the family in Maryland. A lawyer, Richard had no farming skills but could help run the household. Richard also realized he could help slaves escape to Pennsylvania, a free state. On several occasions, Junius had to pay for lost slaves to keep his father out of trouble.

John was only a baby when his grandfather died, but he grew into a man who shared the older man's tendency toward political extremism.

John lived his early years at the farm. He began his education at the local one-room schoolhouse. He was not a strong student. As one of his classmates recalled, "He was not deficient in intelligence or brains—very much in fact the other way—but he was not ... devoted to his studies."[4] Transferring to Bel Air Academy did not help. John had a tough time with memorization, spelling, and math. His sister Asia said of him, "He had to plod. His was not a quickly receptive mind."[5]

Although John did not like school, he was popular. He rode horses well and enjoyed spending time by the stables. He liked to play cards and generally loved excitement. One of his classmates described him as "a wild and impetuous youth."[6] Junius tried to channel his son's energy into something productive—furniture making. John made some beautiful pieces, including a lovely sewing table for his mother. It had inlaid wood, carvings, and other ornamentations.

In 1845, Junius bought a second home in Baltimore. John was seven. Compared to the older Booth children, John's upbringing was more of a combination of rural and city life.

With his sister Asia, John attended a small school where was known for being "argumentative and fervid in debate."[7] But he also liked dogs, butterflies, lightening bugs, and, of course,

John Wilkes Booth began his education in a one-room schoolhouse where children of all grades learned together.

horses. Yet, he displayed a cruel streak toward cats. He "had a mania for killing cats and went about it with enthusiasm that was quite remarkable."[8]

The Booth family's life changed dramatically in 1846 after Adelaide, the wife Junius had abandoned twenty-five years earlier, reappeared. Mary Ann knew about Junius's previous marriage but thought he had divorced. Adelaide came to the United States to claim her rights and make it clear that the *only* legal Booth offspring was her son, Richard.

Adelaide filed for divorce on the grounds of desertion, and Junius ultimately paid a settlement. However, the process took a long time. Adelaide remained in the United States for the residency period required for divorce. During this time, she tormented Mary Ann. Adelaide's divorce from Junius was legalized May 10, 1851, John's thirteenth birthday. Junius and Mary Ann married that same day.

John continued his education at the Milton Academy for Boys, a boarding school in Sparks, Maryland. He repeated the same pattern there, proving to be popular and good at physical activities but a disengaged student. It looked like John might end up someone who could not focus well enough to succeed.

He and his father clashed, but Junius left home a lot, and Mary Ann strongly influenced her son. She told John he had potential but needed to work hard to develop it. His mother's words moved him.

Education in the Nineteenth Century

Abraham Lincoln and John Wilkes Booth represent the extremely different types of educational opportunities available to children in nineteenth-century America. Whereas Lincoln received a scant formal education with teachers of various training backgrounds and students of all ages combined, Booth attended private schools with well-educated teachers and students divided into classes based on age.

According to the 1840 census, only about 55 percent of children between the ages of five and fifteen went to school. Some families needed their children to do farm work; others could not afford school expenses. The opportunity for a child to get an education varied widely depending on the family's income and whether they lived in a city or rural area.

Even after educational reform, only 72 percent of children attended school in 1910. Eight years passed before every state required children to complete elementary school. No schooling beyond that was mandated.

ABRAHAM LINCOLN and JOHN WILKES BOOTH

Because the Milton Academy only taught boys up to age thirteen, John continued his education at St. Timothy's Hall, a military boarding school. Boys wore uniforms and could not use vulgar language, eat food from home, read novels, and sing in one's room, among many other activities.

There, John still struggled academically but excelled in giving presentations, debating, and performing dramatic readings. His peers described him as cheerful and eager to make a name for himself.

In 1851, Junius started building a large home called Tudor Hall. Around this time, the eldest Booth son, June, returned to Maryland. He had been managing a theater in San Francisco and convinced his father and brother Edwin that they could make a fortune acting out West. So, Junius and Edwin accompanied him to California in 1852. After a successful acting tour, Junius began his journey home but died November 30, 1852, on a Mississippi riverboat. He'd developed an infection.

> *A favorite idea that Booth had was that the world needed to be made free of tyrants.*

Mary Ann traveled to Cincinnati, Ohio, to retrieve her husband's remains. She arrived in Baltimore with his body on December 19, 1853. As was customary at the time, Junius was waked at home, an experience that disturbed John, only fourteen.

Man of the House

The Booth family took a serious financial hit after Junius's death. Not having his salary hurt. Plus, they still owed money on Tudor Hall. Mary Ann knew they had to live differently to survive. She rented out their Baltimore home and moved the family to

BOOTH'S EARLY YEARS

the farm. They had around eighty acres of farmland, a small vineyard, milk cows, fenced fields, and a productive garden. Mary Ann thought they could use the land to make a living.

John worked the farm hard. Sometimes he returned home so tired that he skipped eating, washing up to go straight to bed. Because he was the eldest boy at Tudor Hall, John felt he had to be the "man of the house." But he still managed to have a social life. He went to picnics, fairs, hunting trips, and other events. He also visited Baltimore to see some of his city friends.

John also began to develop some political views. He was anti-immigrant and viewed America as a white man's country. He wanted blacks out and said slavery was a blessing.

Despite the Booths work on the farm, it didn't make money. Their inexperience, difficulty hiring reliable help, lack of money, and bad weather all contributed to the problem. Edwin returned

In the nineteenth century, farming was very physically demanding. People and animals did all the labor. Working his family's farm proved difficult for the young John Wilkes Booth.

ABRAHAM LINCOLN and JOHN WILKES BOOTH

Five years older than brother John, Edwin Booth paused his acting career to help his family with their financial problems.

BOOTH'S EARLY YEARS

Edwin Booth (1833–1893)

In 1864, Edwin Booth appeared with his brothers June and John in *Julius Caesar*. Edwin played Brutus, June played Cassius, and John was Marc Antony. The proceeds from this performance helped to pay for a statue of William Shakespeare in New York City's famous Central Park. The statue is still there.

Widely considered the best nineteenth-century actor, Edwin Booth performed throughout the United States and Europe in Shakespearean plays. Hamlet was his signature role. He also managed theaters in New York and Philadelphia. Later in life, he founded the Players, a private club for artists. His contributions to theater are legendary, but his accomplishments are often eclipsed because his name inevitably brings to mind John Wilkes Booth, presidential assassin.

---

to Maryland in 1856 to take charge. He decided to make money to help his family. Like his father, Edwin was a successful actor who could command a good salary.

Edwin also sold the cattle and rented the farm. The Booth family returned to their Baltimore home. John agreed with this decision, since he wanted an acting career, not a farmer's life.

John made his acting debut in 1855. He played Richmond in *Richard III*. His performance went well and made him determined to be a professional actor.

John Sleeper Clarke, lead comedian at the Arch Theatre in Philadelphia, Pennsylvania (and Asia Booth's future husband), promised to get John a job there. Then nineteen, John arrived in Philly in 1857 to begin work as a member of the company.

Chapter 3

NEW SALEM AND THE PRESIDENCY

When Abraham Lincoln returned to New Salem in July 1831, he was twenty-two years old—strong, muscular, and 6 feet 4 inches (193 cm) tall. He took on odd jobs to support himself. He had no difficulty finding work because people liked him, and he was a reliable, hard worker who told great stories. In September 1831, Offutt's store finally opened, and Lincoln landed his first job that did not require physical labor.

Starting Out in New Salem

Lincoln wanted to continue his education. With the help of local schoolmaster, Mentor Graham, he did. He borrowed books about grammar and other basic subjects from Graham. He also studied law.

Lincoln liked to attend local court proceedings and learned how to draw up simple legal documents. He borrowed books from James Rutledge, founder of the New Salem Debating Society. Rutledge invited Lincoln to join the society. Lincoln accepted, revealing himself to be a talented debater.

His boss, Offutt, boasted to all who would listen that Lincoln was both the smartest and strongest man in New Salem. This claim reached the ears of the Clary's Grove gang, a group of

NEW SALEM AND THE PRESIDENCY

men known for shenanigans. The toughest of the gang, Jack Armstrong, challenged Lincoln to a wrestling match, and he agreed.

Many people gathered to see the match, but it's not clear who won. Lincoln showed everyone that he was strong and courageous. And afterward, the Clary's Grove gang became his loyal supporters.

Lincoln acted shy around girls his age, but married women really liked him. They cooked him meals and mended his clothes. Something about Lincoln made these women nurture him.

Even though he'd only been in New Salem for less than a year, Lincoln developed such a great reputation that James Rutledge encouraged him to run for the state legislature. Lincoln had experience navigating the Sangamon River, and New Salem residents knew that their community's success rested on steamboat traffic coming down the Sangamon. Lincoln planned to improve the river, so it would get more boat traffic.

As campaigning started, Lincoln found himself jobless when Offutt's store failed. Around the same time, the Black Hawk War broke out. Lincoln volunteered for the militia, especially since he needed a job.

The Black Hawk War was a dispute involving Chief Black Hawk and other American Indians, including the Sauks, Meskwakis, and Kickapoos, attempting to resettle their land in Illinois. The government said the land wasn't theirs, so Chief Black Hawk and his group tried to take it back in April 1832. They later surrendered.

When Lincoln joined the militia, the men in his company elected him captain. His first sergeant was none other than Jack Armstrong. Years later, as an experienced politician, Lincoln said his election as captain was "a success which gave me more pleasure than any I have had since."[1]

ABRAHAM LINCOLN and JOHN WILKES BOOTH

In 1831, Chief Black Hawk, a member of the Sauk tribe, led warriors of several tribes in an unsuccessful attempt to reclaim their native land. He surrendered to Jefferson Davis.

NEW SALEM AND THE PRESIDENCY

Lincoln did not see action during the Black Hawk War. He recalled experiencing only "a good many bloody struggles with the mosquitoes."[2] Still out of a job, Lincoln reenlisted twice, so he could continue earning a military salary.

Lincoln returned to New Salem two weeks before the election. He campaigned vigorously during that period but still lost. He earned 277 out of the 300 New Salem votes. He was too unknown to have won support elsewhere in the district.

Soon, Lincoln got a job opportunity, an offer of partnership in another general store. William Berry took Lincoln's word that he would eventually earn the money to pay for his share of the business. Unfortunately, neither Lincoln nor Berry handled the business well, so it failed. Now, Lincoln was unemployed and in debt. He worked for years to pay off this debt, and when Berry died in 1835, Lincoln paid his debts, too.

New Salem townspeople rallied to find Lincoln work. He landed two positions: New Salem postmaster and deputy county surveyor. The first job paid fifty-five dollars a year, and the second one required Lincoln to learn how to survey. He supplemented his income by chopping wood, splitting rails, and doing legal work.

In 1834, Lincoln ran once again for the state legislature. He campaigned hard throughout the entire district, saying little about his political goals. People thought he was smart and trusted him because he'd done so much hard labor. He won the election on August 4.

Lincoln went to Vandalia, then capital of Illinois, to assume office. But he had to borrow money to buy a suit. He listened carefully as he learned how the legislature worked and went on to win reelection campaigns in 1836, 1838, and 1840. During his four terms in the legislature, Lincoln was known to be an intelligent, honest, and skillful politician. He belonged to the Whig Party, which favored modernization of banking, urbanization, and government funding for infrastructure improvements like the railroads.

Lincoln's first term in the legislature got even better when he reconnected with John Todd Stuart. Elected at the same time as Lincoln, Stuart had served with Lincoln in the Black Hawk War. Stuart was a college-educated lawyer with a thriving law practice in Springfield, Illinois. Stuart knew that Lincoln was interested in the law and lent him law books. He encouraged Lincoln to study to become a lawyer, which Lincoln did with a single-minded intensity. He was completely self-taught: "I studied with nobody,"[3] he said. Lincoln became licensed to practice law in 1837. He also moved to Springfield, the new Illinois capital, and became a junior partner in Stuart's firm.

A New Beginning

Lincoln arrived in Springfield in April 1837. He rode in on a borrowed horse with all of his belongings in two saddlebags. He first stopped at the general store, where he asked one of the proprietors, Joshua Speed, how much it would cost to purchase a single mattress, sheets, and a pillow. Speed replied that the total would be $17. Lincoln explained that he did not have much money and asked if he could have credit until Christmas. Lincoln further explained that he was trying to be a lawyer and warned Speed that if he failed, he could probably never pay the bill.

Fortunately, Speed knew Lincoln by reputation and offered him a way to avoid debt. He said, "I have a large room with a double bed up-stairs, which you are welcome to share with me."[4] Lincoln accepted this offer and brought in his saddlebags: "Well, Speed, I am moved!"[5] Speed stands out as probably Lincoln's only intimate friend in life. Lincoln and Speed shared a bed for almost four years.

An important part of Lincoln's new job was "riding the circuit," meaning being a traveling lawyer for his district. He

NEW SALEM AND THE PRESIDENCY

Speed and Lincoln lived together as young men and remained close friends throughout their lives. Here is Speed with his wife, Fanny, about twenty years into their forty-year marriage.

really enjoyed this travel, which also enabled him to meet lots of potential voters. While he enjoyed being a lawyer, Lincoln remained interested in a political career. By practicing law and serving in the legislature, he was on a path that allowed him to pursue his ambitions.

Slavery stood out as one of the major issues of the day. Like many other Northerners, Lincoln opposed slavery. However,

> *Slavery was by far the most divisive issue of Lincoln's era.*

for most of the 1830s, he was not very politically involved in fighting the institution. This changed in 1837.

Abolitionists, people who thought slavery immoral, wanted slavery to be ended, or abolished. But some Northerners worried that freed slaves would move to the region and take their jobs. On the other hand, Southerners worried that the abolition movement would lead slaves to overthrow slaveholders. Southern states asked Northern states to join them in their effort to stop abolitionists. In January 1837, the Illinois State Legislature passed a resolution stating that owning slaves was a constitutional right, and abolitionists were dangerous. Only six out of eighty-three lawmakers voted against the resolution. Lincoln was one of them. This marked his first political act against slavery.

Lincoln always disagreed with the practice but hadn't opposed it to the extreme. In 1837, for example, he did not favor citizenship for blacks. Lincoln also found abolitionists too radical. Throughout his life, Lincoln thought the most effective approach to sensitive subjects was "reason, cold, calculating, unimpassioned reason."[6]

Joshua Speed remained Lincoln's best friend. In the evenings, Speed, Lincoln, and their friends would often share stories and discuss politics. Some historians believe Lincoln and Speed had a romantic relationship. Others disagree. Whatever the nature of their relationship, after years together, Lincoln and Speed reached a stage where they thought they should find wives.

Lincoln did not have a great track record with women. Some people say that Lincoln fell in love with Ann Rutledge, the daughter of James Rutledge. It certainly appears that the two were close, and when Ann died of typhoid fever in 1835, Lincoln

NEW SALEM AND THE PRESIDENCY

grew depressed. But there's no evidence the two of them were planning marriage.

In 1836, Lincoln courted Mary Owens, and they made plans to marry. However, both of them had doubts, and the relationship ended in 1837. Two years later, Lincoln met Mary Todd. Like Lincoln's, her family came from Kentucky. Unlike his, her family members included wealthy slaveholders. Because she was lively and attractive, many men tried to woo Todd. But she fancied Lincoln. She thought he was destined for greatness.

Lincoln and Todd shared many similarities. They both lost their mothers as children. They had strong personalities and mood swings. Both loved poetry and politics as well.

Lincoln proposed marriage in 1840, and Todd accepted. But Lincoln changed his mind a few weeks later. He was so distraught after their breakup that friends worried he might harm himself.

Lincoln's Melancholy

People who knew Lincoln well often described him as deeply sad. More than once, friends worried that he might hurt himself. He even spoke of suicide. Lincoln had two emotional breakdowns: one in 1835 and a second in 1841. Historians and clinicians think Lincoln suffered from depression.

People perceived depression, or melancholy, differently in Lincoln's era. The public knew that depression caused suffering, but they also thought it led to certain advantages. They thought depression enhanced a person's capacity for depth, wisdom, and empathy. Some historians argue that Lincoln led an extraordinary life *because* of his melancholy, not in spite of it.

ABRAHAM LINCOLN and JOHN WILKES BOOTH

Famous photographer Matthew Brady took this picture of Mary Todd Lincoln in 1861, when she was First Lady.

NEW SALEM AND THE PRESIDENCY

Right after Lincoln's broken engagement, Speed left Illinois and moved back to Kentucky, where his family lived. Losing his friend was almost too much for Lincoln. He became profoundly depressed. In August 1841, Lincoln went to see Speed. The visit lifted Lincoln's spirits and helped Speed address his own fears about marriage.

When Lincoln broke off their engagement, Todd told him she would wait. And she did for more than a year. Lincoln returned to Springfield, and they renewed their courtship. They married on November 4, 1842. Lincoln was thirty-three and Mary, twenty-three.

The newlyweds moved into a room at the Globe Tavern, a boarding house that while respectable, was not the best. The tavern was probably the nicest place Lincoln had ever lived. For Todd, it was a step down. It was the first time in her life that she had no personal servants. The couple welcomed son Robert Todd Lincoln nine months after they married.

The Lincolns looked for another place to live, but money was tight. Besides supporting his wife and son, Lincoln also gave money to his father. So, they could only manage to rent a small house. Lincoln's father-in-law visited to meet his new grandson. He saw the Lincolns struggling and gave his daughter a $120 annual allowance until he died. As he did for his other married children, he also gave his daughter eighty acres of Illinois land. In 1844, the Lincolns bought a small house in Springfield.

The year before his marriage, Lincoln dissolved his law partnership with Stuart, since both men spent much time on politics. Lincoln became law partners with Stephen Logan. For the next few years, Lincoln continued studying and became an increasingly effective attorney. But in 1844, Logan and Lincoln dissolved their partnership because Logan wished to go into business with his son. Lincoln decided to set up his own firm and asked William (Billy) Herndon to join him as a junior partner. Mary Todd Lincoln and Billy Herndon hated each other.

Lincoln continued riding the circuit throughout his legal career. The district he covered included about 11,000 square miles (17,702 sq km). It took approximately ten weeks to complete the circuit, and Lincoln did so twice yearly. This meant he spent long periods of time away from home. Traveling proved hard on his family life, but he earned a good salary, $150 weekly, after he paid his expenses.

In 1845, Lincoln ran for a seat in the US Congress. He won his seat in 1846, the year that his second son, Edward, was born. When Congress convened the following year, he traveled to Washington, DC, with his family. The Lincolns lived in a boarding house with other congressmen. They tried living in one room, but the boys were loud and rowdy.

The children's behavior displeased the boarders. Although Lincoln worked most of the time, his wife had little else to do except manage her sons. By spring, she decided to move, along with her children, to her father's Kentucky home. With Mary and the children gone, Lincoln devoted himself to work.

Lincoln served on many committees during his term in Congress. The sole Whig in Congress from Illinois, he lacked political allies and didn't have much legislative success. But his time in Washington strengthened his antislavery views. Washington had a population at that time of forty thousand, including two thousand slaves and eight thousand free blacks. Lincoln wrote a bill that would have outlawed slavery there. He could not find other sponsors, so the bill was never brought up for a vote.

After Lincoln's term in Congress ended in 1849, he and his family returned to Springfield. He took a break from political office and focused on his law practice from 1849 to 1854.

NEW SALEM AND THE PRESIDENCY

Personal Losses, Political Gains

A Chicago law firm offered Lincoln a position, but he turned it down. Settling back home in Springfield benefited Lincoln both personally and professionally. His law practice grew more successful, and he and Herndon moved to a bigger office. Lincoln continued to ride the circuit, and Billy took care of business in the office. Lincoln enjoyed the circuit because it gave him time alone and the opportunity to socialize with other men. Time on the circuit also gave him a periodic break from his marriage. While the Lincolns were devoted to each other, their temperaments clashed. Abraham was unaffectionate, and Mary was anxious and hot-tempered.

Tragedy visited the family when their son Eddie, just four, died of tuberculosis. Both Lincolns were devastated. Mary shut herself in her bedroom and cried for weeks. She flew into rages. Abraham held together by throwing himself into his work and caring for his wife and remaining son.

Mary gave birth to their third son, William (Willie) Wallace, in December 1850. Just ten months had passed since Eddie's death. Their fourth son, Thomas (Tad), arrived in April 1853. Lincoln had spent so much time away from home when Robert was little that the two weren't close. Lincoln was different with Willie and Tad. Once the railroad came to Illinois, Lincoln was able to come home on weekends, even when on the circuit. This allowed him to spend more time with his children. Lincoln played with Willie and Tad, read to them, carried them on his shoulders, and pulled them around in a wagon. This behavior in a father was so unusual in Lincoln's era that people often commented on his parenting.

Lincoln thought his political career was over, and it might have been except for the growing tension between the North and South. The North was becoming industrialized; it housed most of the larger cities in the country. European immigrants flocked there, and lots of job opportunities opened up in factories and on the railroads. Plus, 90 percent of the goods manufactured in the US came from the North. The South, in contrast, was primarily an agricultural region. But in order to thrive, the North needed roads and railroads to connect states and make business national. The South wanted states to self-govern, fearing a strong federal government with centralized power would lead to slavery's end.

In 1820, the Missouri Compromise balanced the number of free and slave states in the US and banned slavery in the territory that would become Kansas and Nebraska. A legislative move in 1854 unbalanced this compromise and drew Lincoln back into politics. Illinois Senator Stephen Douglas pushed the passage of the Kansas-Nebraska Act, which made slavery legal in this region.

The act angered Lincoln, and he was not alone. The two major political parties, the Democrats and the Whigs, had so much internal disagreement about the issue that many left the Democratic Party, while the Whig Party fell apart. A new party was born: Republicans. Composed of former Democrats, former Whigs, and others, the Republican Party wanted to repeal the Kansas-Nebraska Act. They welcomed ending slavery altogether and recommended the admission of Kansas into the Union as a free state. They also wanted federal support for railroad and road construction. Lincoln became a Republican in 1856.

The heated response to the Kansas-Nebraska Act signaled conflict to come. Proslavery men in Kansas burned down a hotel and destroyed homes and businesses to scare people into accepting slavery. The abolitionist John Brown and his followers killed five proslavery men. And in the US Senate, proslavery Congressman Preston Brooks used his cane to beat antislavery Senator Charles Sumner, almost killing him.

NEW SALEM AND THE PRESIDENCY

In 1857, the US Supreme Court issued the Dred Scott decision, which ruled blacks were not citizens, had no right to sue, and were not included in the Declaration of Independence. This decision is often considered the worst Supreme Court ruling ever.

Lincoln realized he couldn't sit on the sidelines of the slavery debate. He unsuccessfully ran for the Senate in 1855. He ran again in 1858, against Douglas.

Dred Scott (1799–1858)

Slaveholders welcomed the Dred Scott decision while Northerners reviled it. The ruling deepened the rift between the North and South and led up to the march toward war. But just who was Dred Scott?

He was an enslaved man born in Virginia around 1799. In 1818, slaveholder Peter Blow moved to Alabama, taking Scott and his other slaves. In 1830, Blow moved to St. Louis, Missouri, where he sold Scott to Dr. John Emerson, a US army surgeon. Emerson took Scott to the free state of Illinois and then to the free territory of Wisconsin. After living for years in slavery-prohibited areas, Scott was moved to Louisiana when Emerson transferred there. In 1847, Scott sued for his freedom. The case worked its way through the courts, ultimately reaching the US Supreme Court. The high court ruled that all blacks, slave or free, were not US citizens and could not sue in federal court. The ruling also overturned the Missouri Compromise.

The story ended positively for Scott, though. The sons of Peter Blow, Scott's original owner, opposed slavery. They bought Scott and immediately set him free.

Stephen A. Douglas served as Illinois secretary of state, on the Illinois Supreme Court, as a member of the US House of Representatives, and as a US senator.

NEW SALEM AND THE PRESIDENCY

The campaign made history in many ways, setting Lincoln on the path to national recognition. On June 16, 1858, Lincoln delivered one of the most famous speeches in American history. He said, "A house divided against itself cannot stand. I believe this government cannot endure, permanently half slave and half free. I do not expect the Union to be dissolved—I do not expect the house to fall—but I do expect it will cease to be divided. It will become all one thing or the other."[7]

Douglas tried to convince people that Lincoln was a radical abolitionist and that political issues shouldn't be decided on moral grounds. Lincoln challenged Douglas to a series of debates. Between August and October, they met seven times. Thousands of people came to hear and see Lincoln and Douglas square off. The two men could not have been more different. Douglas was short and stocky—his nickname was the "Little Giant." He wore fancy clothes and spoke dramatically with a deep voice. Lincoln was tall, thin, and dressed plainly. He spoke in a high-pitched voice. The newspapers covered the debates like they were sporting events.

Ultimately, Lincoln lost the election and once again presumed his political career was over. He could not have been more wrong. Exposure from the campaign made him the Republican Party's leader.

On February 27, 1860, Lincoln spoke at Cooper Union Hall in New York City. He talked about slavery logically and without emotion. His speech was well received, and he followed it with additional speeches throughout New England. When the Republican National Convention met in Chicago on May 18, 1860, delegates chose Lincoln as their party's presidential nominee.

Chapter 4

POLITICS AND ACTING

John Wilkes Booth earned eight dollars weekly at the Arch Theatre in the summer of 1857. His work entailed showing up to daily rehearsals and performing in the roles assigned to him. He wanted to be listed on playbills as J. B. Wilkes to prove that he could succeed on his own, since the Booths were a famous theater family.

Junius Booth had distinguished himself as one of the greatest actors of his generation. And Edwin Booth was also an acclaimed actor. Booth didn't want people to compare his acting to theirs in case he flopped.

The Arch Theatre

Twenty-nine men and women made up the Arch Theatre's stock company. Each of these actors had to learn many parts every week. Like many novice actors, Booth had stage fright and sometimes butchered his lines. At other times, he performed skillfully.

One evening, Booth played Lucrezia Borgia and had to deliver his line: "Madam, I am Petruchio Pandolfo." What came out was, "Madam, I am Pondolfio Pet—Pedoflio Pat—Pantuchio Pet—dammit! Who am I?"[1] The audience laughed and though

POLITICS AND ACTING

initially mortified, Booth laughed along. Still, his mistakes embarrassed him. He desperately longed to make a name for himself: "I must have fame!"[2]

When Booth first moved to Philadelphia, he lived with John Sleeper Clarke and Clarke's mother. Before long, he relocated to a boarding house. Like Booth, the other residents hoped to find professional success. Unlike Booth, they knew it took hard work to accomplish goals. One of the boarders said of him, "He was not without ability and might, with study, have succeeded in earning a reputation in his profession; but he was both lazy and inordinately vain."[3]

Theater in the 1800s

Change swept nineteenth-century theater. The growth of cities and higher standards of living increased theater audiences. Improved transportation made it possible for people to get to the theater and for theater companies to travel nationally.

In the early 1800s, society considered acting a sinful practice and shunned performers. Audiences, who watched the show from an open pit, were loud and unruly. This matched the performances they watched, which leaned toward the melodramatic.

By the time Booth began his acting career, the public's perception of the theater had improved. They regarded actors as respectable. Also, audiences were more genteel, and theaters had many amenities, including comfortable seats. Acting styles became more realistic.

Still, life for Booth and other theater professionals of his era was not easy. Travel was challenging, and performance schedules were quite demanding.

ABRAHAM LINCOLN and JOHN WILKES BOOTH

This picture of John Wilkes Booth at age twenty-one shows his attention to clothes and grooming; they highlighted his attractive appearance.

POLITICS AND ACTING

Booth often showed up late to rehearsals, did not study his lines, or try to improve himself. Booth, however, made friends easily. His peers described him as handsome and charming. They also said he was kind and hospitable.

Booth left the Arch Theatre in June 1858. Acting troupes usually halted performances during summer because it got so hot inside that people wouldn't be comfortable in an indoor theater. Booth summered in Niagara Falls with two siblings and a family friend. The vacation gave Booth a chance to contemplate his next move.

The Marshall Theatre

Booth returned to Baltimore. He did not have a steady job, and he and Edwin decided to appear together in a production of *Richard III*. It marked the first time the brothers acted together. Edwin played the title role, Richard III, and Booth played the supporting role, Richmond. The performances of both Booths won praise. Edwin enjoyed his younger brother's work and wrote to their niece Blanche about it, "I think he will make a good actor."[4]

Fortunately, Booth did not have to wait long to get a job for the next theater season. He joined the ensemble company of the Marshall Theatre in Richmond, Virginia. Now earning eleven dollars per week, Booth still insisted on being billed as J. B. Wilkes. He played many small roles at the Marshall.

Richmond suited Booth. He expanded his social circle beyond the theater, with Richmond's leading citizens welcoming him into their homes. But working in the ensemble was grueling. Each night, Booth acted in one or two new plays and had to constantly learn lines. Aware of what he considered the "family curse," Booth avoided alcohol and took his work more seriously than he had at Arch.

An incident on stage revealed his capacity for quick thinking and a "show-must-go-on" attitude. During a performance, the actress Kate Fisher got too close to the gas footlights of the stage, and her skirt caught on fire. Hearing cries for help from the audience, Booth immediately extinguished the fire. They continued their performance as if nothing happened.

During the 1858–59 theatrical season, Booth performed once more with his brother Edwin, this time in *Hamlet*. Once again, Edwin played the title role, and Booth played the supporting role, Horatio. The performance was a hit. A proud Edwin pointed his brother out to the audience and asked, "I think he's done well, don't you?"[5] The audience cheered and shouted, "Yes! Yes!"[6] Booth performed in eighty-three plays in 1858. Of all the Shakespearean characters he played, he liked Brutus from *Julius Caesar* best because he killed a tyrant.

His strong melodious voice made Booth memorable as an actor. He had a gift for elocution, or clear speaking. While he certainly had innate talent, Booth worked hard to improve his craft. His diligence paid off, as the Marshall Theatre hired him for a second season. Booth scored better parts, including leads.

Booth's experience in Richmond intensified his positive feelings about the South. He liked Virginia better than Maryland or Pennsylvania, where he'd also lived. He found that Southerners welcomed actors more than Northerners. Also, in Virginia, Booth was permitted to court elite young women.

> *John Wilkes Booth felt welcomed by Southern society. He thought of himself as a Southerner.*

When the North and South differed on a topic, including slavery, Booth favored the Southern position. He told his sister Asia that he wanted "to be

POLITICS AND ACTING

loved by the Southern people above all things."[7] In 1859, Booth got his first chance to prove his faithfulness to the South.

Abolitionist John Brown fought hard to end slavery. He helped slaves escape through the Underground Railroad in Pennsylvania and fought to keep Kansas free. In October 1859, John Brown and his followers took over the federal arsenal in Harper's Ferry, Virginia. In doing so, they gained access to a supply of weapons, which Brown planned to use for a slave revolt. But the Virginia militia surrounded the arsenal and recaptured it after a fierce battle with Brown and his men, ten of whom died in the fight. Brown survived, but the authorities arrested him. He was convicted of treason and sentenced to hanging.

While Southerners viewed Brown as a criminal, Northerners considered him a hero, so concern grew that Northerners might rescue him. The Virginia militia headed to Charlestown, where Brown was being held. Booth was on break at the theater when

US Abolitionism

Abolitionists had one goal: to set slaves free. The first attempt to end slavery in America can be found in the antislavery language of the earliest draft of the Declaration of Independence. Unfortunately, other delegates of the Continental Congress removed this language.

After the Revolutionary War ended, Northern states abolished slavery. Vermont became the first to do so in 1777. Thirty years later, importing enslaved Africans into the United States was outlawed, and the Missouri Compromise of 1820 limited slavery. In the South, however, slavery thrived.

The North and South could not compromise on the issue. Abolitionists maintained it was impossible to reach an agreement because slavery was a moral abomination. They said freedom for all people was the only solution.

ABRAHAM LINCOLN and JOHN WILKES BOOTH

John Brown is shown here in an 1846 photo. He holds the flag of the Subterranean Pass-Way, his planned expansion of the Underground Railroad into the Deep South.

POLITICS AND ACTING

he saw the militia, known as the Grays, lining up to board a train to guard Brown.

Booth considered Brown "a cutthroat and murderer"[8] and enjoyed discussing possible punishments for him. On impulse, Booth talked his way into joining the Grays. They gave him a uniform, and he boarded the train. But Booth didn't tell his employer that he was leaving, and since he was a popular actor in the theater company, management was furious when they found out.

Accompanied by the Governor of Virginia, the Grays left Richmond. They first went to Washington and marched past the White House in a deliberate act of intimidation. Next, they boarded a train to Charlestown along with several other militia companies. Altogether, about 1,200 men arrived in Charlestown, nearly doubling their population. The militia stayed for two weeks, and with so many armed men guarding him, Brown would not escape.

The abolitionist was hanged on December 2, 1859. The militia formed lines around the scaffold, and Booth had a close view of the event. He watched John Brown walk onto the platform. He saw Brown's calm face. While Booth felt proud that he'd helped stop Brown from escaping, he felt faint when he saw the abolitionist hanging. Booth thought Brown deserved to die but admired his courage. He told his sister Asia, "He was a brave old man; his heart must have broken when he felt himself deserted."[9]

Booth returned to Richmond on December 4, 1859. His manager fired him for leaving without notice. However, Booth was not jobless for long. Several militiamen went to the theater to insist Booth keep his job, and many theatergoers wrote letters of support. The manager caved; Booth finished the 1859–60 season.

ABRAHAM LINCOLN and JOHN WILKES BOOTH

Leading Man

After two years at the Marshall Theatre, Booth wanted a change. Canning's Dramatic Company hired him to go on tour as a star actor. They opened the season in Columbus, Georgia, with *Romeo and Juliet*. Booth starred as Romeo. The company then moved to Montgomery, Alabama, and many other cities. Booth took on a new lead character six nights a week, making good money. At his peak, Booth earned an annual salary of $20,000. That's more than $500,000 today.

Then, after a terrible mishap, he was derailed. Somehow Canning accidentally shot Booth in the thigh. The injury was serious but not life threatening. A physician sewed up the wound, leaving the bullet in the leg, as surgery was too risky. Booth had a four-month recovery that stopped him from performing. Canning paid Booth's bills but did not hire him for the next season.

While Booth recuperated from his injury, the country buzzed about the upcoming presidential election. Four men were running. The Southern Democrats nominated John C. Breckinridge, who favored both states' rights and slavery. The Northern Democrats chose Stephen Douglas, who thought the Union should be preserved and that the nation could compromise on slavery. The Constitutional Union Party nominated John Bell. He supported slavery where it existed but opposed expanding it. Finally, the Republican Party nominated Abraham Lincoln, who supported the preservation of the Union and opposed the spread of slavery.

Booth saw Douglas speak in Montgomery and ultimately deemed him a professional politician and opportunist. This left Booth in a tough spot politically. He appreciated states' rights but did not want the Union dissolved. He opposed secession as strongly as he did abolition. His feelings on the matter were intense: "If I could I would kill every d___ Abolitionist in the North and every d___ secessionist in the South, then there would

POLITICS AND ACTING

This image parodies the 1860 presidential race and its four candidates: Breckenridge (*upper left*), Lincoln (*upper right*), Bell (*lower right*), and Douglass.

be no war. This is too grand a country to be plunged in to civil war by such fanatics!"[10]

Then living in Montgomery, Alabama, Booth freely shared his opinions about politics. He thought Southerners had the right to own slaves and that the Southern way of life should be respected. Such views were met with approval. Booth also spoke against secession, endangering his life in the process.

Canning helped him leave Montgomery on December 3, 1860. After taking a train to Savannah, Georgia, Booth boarded a steamer to New York City, Edwin's home. He arrived December 9, 1860, worried about living with his brother and his "Northern views."

Chapter 5

THE PRESIDENTIAL ELECTION

After winning the Republican Party's nomination for president, Lincoln had to face the three other candidates nominated by their parties. Unable to agree among themselves, the Democratic Party divided into groups representing Northern Democrats and Southern Democrats. In addition, the Constitutional Union Party formed. That party expressed no political views other than that it wished to preserve the Union and considered the Constitution its guide.

Today, the Democratic and Republican parties are the nation's two major political parties, and running for president completely differs from what it was like in 1860. For example, Lincoln did not give speeches, travel, or campaign on his own behalf during the presidential race. And except for giving one speech, neither did John C. Breckinridge of the Southern Democrats. John Bell of the Constitutional Union Party said nothing. Only Stephen Douglas, of the Northern Democrats, broke with tradition, traveling all over the nation giving speeches and meeting voters himself.

Running for President

While most of the presidential candidates stayed off the campaign trail, this does not mean they didn't send out others to

THE PRESIDENTIAL ELECTION

represent them. Quite the contrary—they deployed hundreds of people to convince voters to support their candidacy. Lincoln's representatives had a lot of work to do. His rivals said some awful things, calling him ugly and unintelligent. Worse, many fanned the flames of racism and spread rumors that if Lincoln was elected, he'd force blacks and whites to marry.

As a result of the smear campaign, the South hated Lincoln so much that his name didn't appear on the election ballot there. Lincoln's supporters tried to rehab his image. They characterized him as honest and hardworking. The Republicans held a lot of rallies on Lincoln's behalf. They also organized voter registration drives, winning over young people drawn to the Republican Party because it was new and to Lincoln because he was different.

Lincoln's campaign posters featured him and running mate, Hannibal Hamlin, one of Maine's most influential politicians. Hamlin was a US senator before and after his time as vice president.

ABRAHAM LINCOLN and JOHN WILKES BOOTH

Even though Lincoln did not travel to campaign, he met many potential voters. After his nomination, seemingly *everyone* wanted to a chance to see him. At first, he welcomed the throngs of visitors to his home, but the crowds soon became unmanageable. Fortunately, Governor John Wood offered Lincoln use of his office in the Illinois state capital.

Lincoln also had a mountain of correspondence to handle, so he hired John Nicolay to serve as his personal secretary. Lincoln's wealthy Springfield friends paid Nicolay's salary. Soon the work became more than Nicolay could manage, leading Lincoln to hire John Hay to help out as well.

John Hay (1838–1905)

John Hay, Lincoln's personal secretary, had the odd distinction of knowing three assassinated presidents: Lincoln, Garfield, and McKinley.

Lincoln, the sixteenth US president, worked seven days a week and did not take vacations. This meant Hay was on call constantly. He even lived in the White House. Lincoln and Hay became so close they developed a father-son relationship. Hay was even at Lincoln's bedside when the president died.

President John Garfield, the twentieth US president, was assassinated after less than a year in office. Hay served as an advisor for Garfield, who wanted him to work as his personal secretary. Hay declined but went on to serve as secretary of state for William McKinley, the twenty-fifth president. After McKinley's assassination, President Theodore Roosevelt asked Hay to stay on as secretary of state, which he did.

John Hay served the nation for more than forty years.

THE PRESIDENTIAL ELECTION

Two secretaries faithfully served Lincoln during his presidency: John Nicolay (*left*) and John Hay (*right*). After Lincoln's death, the two wrote the ten-volume collection *Abraham Lincoln: A History*.

ABRAHAM LINCOLN and JOHN WILKES BOOTH

The fracturing of the Democratic Party made the Republican Party hopeful that Lincoln would win the election. His views about slavery guaranteed support from Northern states. Lincoln did not want to see slavery spread but could not see how to legally stamp out the institution in states where it already existed. He hoped slavery would die out because it would one day be too costly for the South to maintain.

Slavery, though, wasn't the only pressing political issue. The Republicans favored the development of infrastructure. They also favored protective tariffs, fees that people would pay for importing goods from abroad. Republicans argued that tariffs would support the development of industries in the US, since the goods would cost users less than overseas imports. The Republicans thought that protective tariffs would foster economic growth in the South too.

But Southerners disagreed. They opposed tariffs, as they did little manufacturing and imported many goods from abroad. They saw the tariff as an unfair fee with economic drawbacks.

Finally, Election Day arrived. Lincoln hesitated to cast a ballot, thinking it inappropriate to vote for himself. Others convinced him to vote to support other Republican candidates. Lincoln agreed but did not cast a vote for president.

In 1860, election results took time to trickle in, unlike today. Results came in by telegraph, revealing Lincoln as the clear winner. He made history as the first Republican elected president. He won every free state except New Jersey, which he split with Stephen Douglas. Lincoln did not receive a single vote from ten of the slave states.

> *Lincoln ran for president in a deeply divided nation. He received no votes in ten of the slave states.*

THE PRESIDENTIAL ELECTION

Nineteenth-Century Telegraphy

Telegraphy refers to the long-distance transmission of messages without the physical exchange of an object. Email is a modern form of telegraphy. In the nineteenth century, electrical telegraphy was the most hi-tech way to send information. The message sent was called a telegram.

Samuel Morse developed and patented the electrical telegraph in the United States in 1837. Morse and his assistant, Alfred Vail, invented the Morse code—a way to signal letters of the alphabet so they could be sent along wires and then deciphered by the person receiving the message.

Telegraph lines connected cities and towns into a giant network. By 1852, there were twenty telegraph companies with 23,000 miles (37,015 km) of wire. The east and west coasts of America became connected by October 1861.

News of the Civil War was spread through the country via telegraph. This is how Lincoln stayed informed about the latest events.

More than 82 percent of all eligible voters cast ballots. Lincoln won just under 40 percent of the popular vote, since he'd competed with three other candidates. Thus Lincoln had a plurality, not a majority. However, Lincoln did get an overwhelming amount of Electoral College votes. Still used today, the college is a system by which electors cast votes that represent how the people of their state voted. The number of electors a state has depends on population, with more populous states getting more electors. By winning the free Northern states as well as California and Oregon, Lincoln earned 180 Electoral College votes. The other three candidates won 123 combined.

ABRAHAM LINCOLN and JOHN WILKES BOOTH

Once Lincoln learned that he'd won the election, he grew nervous because he now had to run the nation. Trouble came right away. Shortly after the election and months before he took the oath of office to become president, the South made plans to secede from the Union. Northerners didn't know how to react. Some thought the South should be allowed to leave, but many still thought a compromise could be reached. Others disagreed with the idea of a compromise. President Buchanan was unhelpful. He believed secession violated the Constitution but could not prevent it from occurring. All eyes turned to Lincoln.

But Lincoln couldn't do anything either—at least not yet. In December 1860, the month after he won the presidential race, South Carolina seceded from the Union. Mississippi, Florida, and Alabama followed in January 1861. By early February, Georgia, Louisiana, and Texas had seceded too. The South seized the federal military forts in their states. And on February 18, 1861, Jefferson Davis became president of the self-proclaimed Confederate States of America.

Getting Ready to Be President

The South seceded as Lincoln prepared to move to Washington. With the help of Nicolay and Hay in Springfield, Lincoln steadily handled the tasks necessary for the transition. All three men dealt with baskets of correspondence and long lines of visitors who wanted to express their concerns, ask for jobs, or just see the president-elect. Lincoln saw these visitors daily for hours.

Fifty-one years old and energetic, Lincoln loved talking to people. He told jokes and funny stories, sometimes laughing and slapping his leg with amusement. He used stories to break the ice with strangers, deflect criticism, avoid unwelcome questions, and get rid of annoying people.

THE PRESIDENTIAL ELECTION

Jefferson Davis is best known as the Confederate president, but the West Point grad also served as a congressman, US secretary of war, and senator.

During the months between his election and oath of office, Lincoln made no public speeches. He acted cautiously to avoid further alienating the secessionists.

A couple of months before leaving for Washington, Lincoln went to visit his stepmother, Sally. They had a long visit, during which she said she didn't want him to be president because she feared for his safety. He tried to reassure her.

Upon returning to Springfield, Lincoln had several household tasks to complete. He gave his dog, Fido, to a local boy and his horse to a neighbor. He rented out their home. The Lincolns packed their belongings in trunks to send to the White House. Lincoln met with his law partner and told him to leave up their "Lincoln and Herndon" sign because he planned to practice again if he survived his presidency.

Mary Todd Lincoln, excited to be First Lady, bought a new wardrobe. She went on a shopping spree. Finding that merchants were eager to give her credit, she ran up debts that she hid from her husband.

On February 11, 1861, Lincoln and his family, along with Nicolay, Hay, and Ward Hill Lamon, boarded a train to Washington. Lamon was a lawyer friend who served as Lincoln's bodyguard. The entire trip to took more than 1,900 miles (3,058 km). It required traveling on eighteen railroads and lasted twelve days.

As the train passed through several states, including Indiana, Ohio, Pennsylvania, and New York, people cheered. During a stop in Westfield, New York, Lincoln met Grace Bedell, a little girl who had written to him suggesting that he grow his beard. He wanted her to see that he'd followed her advice.

When Lincoln's train arrived in Philadelphia, they learned of an assassination plot in Baltimore. Lincoln didn't know if the threat was real but followed the advice to play it safe. Rather than staying on the train and going to Washington after

THE PRESIDENTIAL ELECTION

Lincoln's contemporaries often remarked that photographs did not capture his lively essence. Here, he is pictured early in his presidency, with his famous beard.

passing through Baltimore, Lincoln left the train and headed to Washington through an alternative route. Because the public knew what Lincoln looked like, he wore a disguise, swapping his trademark stovepipe hat for a felt one. He arrived safely but regretted having to sneak into Washington.

His inauguration took place on March 4, 1861, in front of the Capitol building. Sharpshooters positioned themselves on rooftops looking for would-be assassins. Stephen Douglas stood by Lincoln, holding the new president's hat during the ceremony. Lincoln delivered a thoughtful and carefully worded speech. He said he wished to avoid civil war and urged the states that seceded to rejoin the Union. He also said that he did not intend to abolish slavery in the Southern states, "I have no purpose, directly or indirectly, to interfere with the institution of slavery in the states where it exists. I believe I have no lawful right to do so, and I have no inclination to do so."[1]

Lincoln's words fells on deaf ears. The Southern states refused to rejoin the Union. Conflict appeared inevitable.

Lincoln faced a serious challenge. Major Robert Anderson, the commander of Fort Sumter in South Carolina, reported that he and his men were low on provisions. He asked that they be resupplied. This is a standard request for a military commander to make, but in this case, Confederate troops surrounded the fort. It was not clear how to proceed. Lincoln feared that resupplying the fort would invite a Confederate attack. Yet he did not wish to abandon the fort, so he carefully gathered information. He knew the fate of the Union was at stake and grew determined that it would not surrender any forts. On the other hand, Lincoln did not want the Union to be the first to fire shots.

Lincoln communicated with the governor of South Carolina, informing him that provisions would arrive at the fort. He promised not to send additional men, guns, or ammunition, provided the Confederates did not stop the delivery of food and

THE PRESIDENTIAL ELECTION

related goods. Lincoln was trying to avoid an armed conflict. The governor of South Carolina told Confederate President Davis of Lincoln's plan to deliver supplies to Fort Sumter. Davis demanded the fort's surrender, but Major Anderson refused. Confederate troops opened fire on the fort at 4:30 a.m., April 12, 1861, starting the Civil War. Union soldiers surrendered Fort Sumter two days later.

Lincoln called for seventy thousand militia volunteers. Many in the North joined eagerly. In the South, young men stepped up to fight what they perceived as aggression from the North. Within the next few months, Virginia, North Carolina, Arkansas, and Tennessee seceded. Delaware, Missouri, and Maryland, all slave states, strongly leaned toward secession but remained in the Union. Kentucky tried to remain neutral.

The situation was dire. Both Virginia and Maryland surround Washington. And using a telescope, Lincoln could see the campfires and tents of the nearby Confederate soldiers. Lincoln insisted on preserving the Union and deemed secession illegal. He did not recognize the Confederate States of America as an independent country.

On April 25, 1861, Union troops marched into Washington, providing the first real protection from Confederate attack for Lincoln in his young presidency.

Booth's Reaction

Booth was performing in a series of plays in Albany, New York, when the train carrying Lincoln to Washington stopped there. Lincoln got off to greet the crowd. No one knows if Booth witnessed the meet-and-greet.

In Booth's hotel, he loudly shared his views about the president. He denounced Lincoln and revealed his allegiance

ABRAHAM LINCOLN and JOHN WILKES BOOTH

The famous printing firm Currier and Ives produced this lithograph, or print, depicting the Confederacy attacking Fort Sumter's interior.

THE PRESIDENTIAL ELECTION

to the South. Hotel guests complained to the manager about Booth's remarks.

A news dealer in Albany recalled, "Booth at that time openly and boldly avowed his admiration for the rebels and their deeds, which he characterized as the most heroic of modern times."[2] According to Booth, "The Southern leaders know how to defend their rights and would not submit to oppression."[3]

Despite his reverence for the South, the actor never joined the Confederate army. Years later, his brother Edwin explained that their mother begged Booth not to go to war because four of her children had already died. Booth promised her he would not but regretted this decision.

Chapter 6

THE CIVIL WAR

The shots Confederates fired at Fort Sumter started the military conflict between the North and the South. Each side thought the fighting would end in months. Instead, the Civil War raged on for four years. Estimates of how many died range from roughly 700,000 to more than one million. According to the 1860 census, 8 percent of all whites ages thirteen to forty-three died in the war. The South suffered more casualties, with an 18 percent casualty rate compared to the North's 6 percent casualty rate. The death toll was greater for black soldiers, with about 20 percent losing their lives.

War Begins

Once the war started, Lincoln tried to keep the country intact by ordering the Navy to block Confederate ports with Union ships. He then called for volunteers to serve in the militia and added regiments to expand the army's size. Finally, he suspended the writ of habeas corpus making it possible to arrest Confederate sympathizers. In doing so, Lincoln hoped to minimize the rebellion.

ABRAHAM LINCOLN and JOHN WILKES BOOTH

The Writ of Habeas Corpus

When the founding fathers wrote the Constitution, they included habeas corpus in the first article. Habeas corpus prevents the government from imprisoning a person without showing cause. If someone is arrested, they can challenge their detention by filing a habeas corpus petition. Doing so forces the government to explain to a neutral judge its reasons for incarceration.

Lincoln halted habeas corpus to preserve the country. He maintained that secession was illegal and, therefore, so was the Confederacy. Moreover, he argued that the South still belonged to the Union and was subject to its laws. Lincoln saw the war as a fight to save democracy, "a struggle for maintaining in the world, that form, and substance of government, whose leading object is, to elevate the condition of men ... to afford all, an unfettered start, and a fair chance, in the race of life."[1]

The first major battle of the war, at Bull Run in Virginia, dispelled any notion that the war would be quick. The Union Army suffered a significant loss. Worse, after this battle and throughout 1861 and into 1862, Lincoln had great difficulty finding generals to effectively lead the troops. Even though they greatly outnumbered the Confederate Army, the Union Army could not get traction. This situation changed in 1862, when Lincoln replaced his secretary of war with Edwin Stanton, and General Ulysses S. Grant won some decisive Union victories with his hard-fighting troops.

Pictures of Lincoln before and during the war show the toll that leading a fractured nation had on him. His family life also resulted in turmoil and sadness. Because he was busy

THE CIVIL WAR

Taken in 1864, several years into the war, this photograph shows an older looking and careworn Lincoln.

and distracted, Lincoln had little time to spend with his wife. Emotionally fragile, she depended on his calming influence. Without it, she became agitated and sometimes acted impulsively or erratically. Even the joys of parenting caused strife. Lincoln's small sons Willie and Tad ran around the White House, but people complained that they would burst into meetings and cause mischief.

Lincoln was especially close to Willie because the boy was so much like him. But tragedy struck in February 1862, when Willie and Tad fell ill. Tad improved but Willie got worse. He died of typhoid fever on February 20, 1861. Mary Todd Lincoln was devastated; she did not leave her bed for a month. Lincoln was also heartbroken. He said, "My poor boy, he was too good for this earth … But then we loved him so."[2] Lincoln threw himself into his work, crying when he thought of Willie.

As 1862 unfolded, the war continued, and Lincoln learned about war strategy. He also decided to do something about slavery. He saw thousands of slaves making their way North to freedom and noticed that African Americans, even when free, were treated poorly.

On August 14, 1862, Lincoln held a meeting, the first of its kind, with black leaders at the White House. Lincoln told the group about his intention to end slavery. Noting the terrible treatment of blacks, he proposed separating them from whites to spare them from further racial abuse. Lincoln thought that the voluntary recolonization of blacks to Central America and the Caribbean would solve the problem. Black leaders, however, hated this plan. It angered abolitionist Frederick Douglass.

He questioned why blacks should leave the only home they'd known, the nation their ancestors had lived in for generations. Lincoln quickly came to see how wrong-headed he'd been.

As the war dragged on, Lincoln concluded that for the Union to survive, slavery would have to be destroyed. He wanted to free

THE CIVIL WAR

In 1860, Frederick Douglass was in his prime, already in great demand as a speaker. Lincoln welcomed Douglass's visits to the White House, and they became friends.

Frederick Douglass (1818–1895)

Frederick Douglass is one of the most influential Americans of the nineteenth century. He was born into slavery in 1818 but escaped for good, after two unsuccessful attempts, in 1838. After he fled, Douglass made his way north to Philadelphia, a city that strongly opposed slavery. He then traveled north to New York City to the safe house of abolitionist David Ruggles. Douglass settled in Massachusetts.

But he did not choose a quiet life. He became a writer, orator, abolitionist, and social reformer. He wrote several books, including his autobiography, *Narrative of the Life of Frederick Douglass, an American Slave*. Published in 1845, it became a bestseller, translated into several languages. Some readers could not believe that an uneducated former slave could have written the book. Douglass was self-taught but possessed an ability to write and speak eloquently. Douglass used his gifts to work tirelessly for the freedom and improvement of blacks before, during, and after the Civil War.

---

the slaves, but his advisors recommended waiting until a Union battle victory so that his decision would not look like an act of desperation. The Battle of Antietam gave Lincoln his opportunity.

Within a few days, Lincoln read the Emancipation Proclamation to his cabinet. He signed it on January 1, 1863, "as a fit and necessary war measure, I do order and declare that all persons held as slaves … henceforward shall be free; and that the Executive government of the United States … will recognize and maintain the freedom of said persons."[3]

The proclamation freed slaves only in the states that had seceded from the Union. Predictably, Southerners were outraged. Northerners were split—Republicans were pleased and Democrats less so. Upon signing the proclamation, Lincoln said, "I never, in my life, felt more certain that I was doing right, than I do in signing this paper."[4]

The war intensified in 1863. Lincoln announced a military draft. The Union army could no longer rely on volunteers alone. After the Emancipation Proclamation, the military enlisted former slaves into the army. By the war's end, 180,000 black soldiers had taken part. Lincoln thought it was fitting to let African Americans fight for the Union as well as for the end of slavery. He also thought the sight of black soldiers would unnerve the Confederate troops. He wrote, "The bare sight of 50,000 armed and drilled black soldiers on the banks of the Mississippi would end the rebellion at once."[5]

A Turning Tide

General Robert E. Lee and his Confederate troops invaded Pennsylvania. The battle at Gettysburg stood out as the war's fiercest. The Union forces won, and in July 1863, General Grant captured Vicksburg. The war shifted in the Union's direction.

On November 18, 1863, Lincoln went to Gettysburg to dedicate a military cemetery there. His speech, the Gettysburg Address, was fewer than three hundred words. In it, Lincoln described the war as a fight for liberty and equality for all, including slaves. Lincoln said the soldiers killed fighting had ensured the future of democracy and a "government of the people, by the people, for the people, shall not perish from the earth."[6]

After visiting Gettysburg, Lincoln worked on his plan to reconstruct the Union when the war ended. He issued the Proclamation of Amnesty and Reconstruction in December

ABRAHAM LINCOLN and JOHN WILKES BOOTH

Robert E. Lee served in the US military from 1829 to 1861. He joined the Confederate army when his home state of Virginia seceded from the Union.

THE CIVIL WAR

1863. It stated that the rebels must swear to support the Constitution and the Union. Rebels who promised could keep their property, except for slaves. High-ranking Confederate officials did not qualify for this oath.

Lincoln put Grant, who had a plan to end the war, in charge of all Union troops. Grant warned that the plan would result in numerous deaths, but Lincoln agreed to it. In early 1864, he called for 700,000 more army recruits, and Grant began the Overland Campaign. A brutal war of attrition, the North and the South suffered terrible losses. The North, however, could add more soldiers, while the South lacked reinforcements. Lincoln also gave Grant the authority to destroy Confederate plantations, bridges, and railroads.

As the battles went on, the 1864 presidential election neared. Republicans nominated Lincoln to run for reelection. Democrats nominated George McClellan, one of Lincoln's war generals from early on. The country was so war-weary that Lincoln figured he'd lose the election. However, in September 1864, the Union won the Battle of Atlanta. This helped Lincoln's chances. When the election occurred, Lincoln won definitively. Union soldiers strongly supported him.

After his reelection, Lincoln set out to pass a constitutional amendment to outlaw slavery. Although the Emancipation Proclamation freed slaves, it only did so in the Confederate states. Also, Lincoln realized that the courts might consider the proclamation a temporary wartime measure. A constitutional amendment would permanently prohibit slavery.

> *Lincoln believed that the war was fought to provide liberty for all and to preserve democracy.*

Ulysses S. Grant ultimately led the Union army to victory. Grant was the eighteenth US president, serving two terms from 1869–1877.

THE CIVIL WAR

After much debate, the Thirteenth Amendment passed by a vote of 119 to 56. All states were finally free states. Lincoln viewed the amendment as a moral victory because "if slavery is not wrong, nothing is wrong."[7]

Lincoln's second inauguration took place on March 4, 1865. He made a very short speech, saying of the war, "All dreaded it—all sought to avert it … but one of them would make war rather than let the nation survive; and the other would accept war rather than let it perish."[8] Lincoln wanted to heal the nation and forge lasting peace. He would not punish the rebels but wished to proceed "with malice toward none."[9]

The war ground on. Grant kept advancing, wearing Lee down. Union troops surrounded Richmond, the Confederate capital. Richmond fell into Union hands on April 3, 1865.

Six days later, Lee surrendered to Grant at the Appomattox Court House. Shortly afterward, Lincoln spoke to a crowd at the White House about rebuilding the nation. He also suggested giving blacks voting rights. Booth stood in the crowd angrily listening to Lincoln.

Booth's War

When the war began, Booth hit his stride as an actor, earning lots of money. While not on stage, he visited his brother Edwin. But these visits were tense, as they could not talk about politics or the war without fighting.

In April 1863, Booth began the spring theater season in Washington. After that, he performed in Missouri, where he and fellow actor T. L. Connor were arrested for making treasonous remarks about Lincoln. Connor was sentenced to sixty days in a military prison. Booth agreed to take an oath of allegiance to the Union and pay a fine to avoid jail.

As the Union emerged as victor, Booth's emotions intensified. He was on a train with brother-in-law John Sleeper Clarke, when Clarke criticized Confederate President Jefferson Davis. Booth grabbed his throat and said, "Never, if you value your life, never speak in that way again of a man and a cause I hold sacred."[10]

Booth also smuggled goods into the South. In particular, he brought quinine, needed for soldiers with malaria. Booth used his acting money to finance this operation.

In November 1863, Booth performed in Washington's new Ford's Theatre. He starred in *The Marble Heart*, playing a romantic, young sculptor. A theater-lover, Lincoln saw Booth in the play. He enjoyed Booth's performance so much that he asked to meet him, but Booth refused.

After Ford's, Booth hit the road again, ending his tour in Boston in April 1864. By July, Booth was meeting with Confederate spies there. He hatched a scheme to help the losing South—he would kidnap Lincoln.

Before black soldiers fought for the Union, the North and South regularly exchanged prisoners of war. Once blacks started fighting, the South said they would treat any they captured as runaway slaves. The North stopped all prisoner exchanges, which disproportionately affected the South because it had fewer men. So, Booth planned to kidnap Lincoln in exchange for every captured rebel.

Booth organized a group to execute his plan. In October 1864, he went to Montreal to see Confederate agents there. Booth stayed for ten days, and historians suspect he got approval and resources for his kidnapping plot.

Booth returned to the US and went to Maryland to figure out the route he and his coconspirators would take to get Lincoln to Virginia. When Booth visited Philadelphia to see his sister Asia, his hatred of Lincoln frightened her. Booth railed, "He is made the tool of the North to crush out, or try to crush out, slavery by robbery, rape, slaughter, and bought armies."[11] Booth blamed Lincoln for the South's problems and regretted not taking revenge at his second inauguration. He mused that he had an "excellent chance… to kill the President, if I had wished."[12]

Chapter 7

THE ASSASSINATION

As the Confederacy's situation became increasingly dire, Booth grew despondent and erratic. He wanted to give the Confederacy the chance to fight what, he considered, a valiant battle. Booth believed that before the Civil War the United States was the best country on Earth. He thought Lincoln had ruined it by increasing the federal government's power, emancipating slaves, establishing an income tax, drafting people into the military, and suspending habeas corpus. Booth wanted the president stopped.

Kidnapping Shifts to Revenge

Lincoln's second inauguration pushed Booth to follow through on his kidnapping plot. His coconspirators included Lewis Powell, a Confederate veteran; Davey Herold, who knew the Southern Maryland back roads; and John Surratt, a Confederate smuggler. Boatman George Atzerodt rounded out the group. He would ferry the kidnapping party, including Lincoln, across the Potomac River to Virginia.

Booth bought a Derringer, a small handgun, while waiting for the perfect kidnapping opportunity. He learned that on March 17, the president would visit the South Street Hospital

THE ASSASSINATION

Only twenty-three years old, David Herold was John Wilkes Booth's accomplice in Lincoln's assassination. Here, Herold is shown in the Washington Navy Yard after his arrest.

for a wounded soldiers event. Booth knew that Lincoln would be riding in a carriage, under little, if any, guard, on his way there.

The actor assembled his team, and they rode on horseback toward the hospital. They intended to ride next to Lincoln's carriage and force it roadside. After overpowering the driver, they would restrain Lincoln and drive the carriage to Maryland. Then, they planned to take a boat to Virginia.

Their plan never took off. Lincoln skipped the hospital visit at the last minute. The news disappointed the conspirators, and they decided to give up on kidnapping Lincoln. They feared someone might discover their plot. But Booth still wanted revenge on Lincoln.

Booth could see the Confederacy was near its end. Overwhelmed by anxiety and dismay, he drank heavily. On April 9, General Lee officially surrendered. Millions of Americans celebrated and rejoiced but certainly not Booth.

While Booth saw his future darken, Lincoln saw bright days ahead. The day after Lee's surrender, crowds gathered near the White House. Lincoln cheerfully addressed those gathered

The Confederate Secret Service

Historians don't know the full story of the Confederate Secret Service (CSS) because the Confederate government intentionally destroyed most of the official papers in April 1865 before evacuating Richmond. While the picture may be incomplete, historians do know that the CSS deployed couriers, spies, saboteurs, and even implemented a raid of St. Albans, Vermont, in 1864. The CSS had one goal—to disrupt the Union's execution of the war. It is likely, although not certain, that the CSS supported Booth's plots to kidnap or assassinate Lincoln.

THE ASSASSINATION

and asked the band there to play "Dixie," one of his favorite songs. Composed by a Northerner and appropriated by the Confederacy, Lincoln joked that "Dixie" could be reclaimed as a "lawful prize."

On April 11, Lincoln spoke more seriously to the White House crowd, which included Booth. Two days later, celebratory lights and candles illuminated Washington. It was a spectacular sight.

Good Friday, a holy day for Christians marking the crucifixion of Jesus, fell on the next day. Lincoln woke up feeling calmer and happier than he had in some time. His son Robert arrived home after serving as one of Grant's officers. Robert had been at Appomattox and witnessed Lee's surrender. He told his father about it over breakfast.

Afterward, Lincoln went out with his wife and Tad and then returned to the White House for a cabinet meeting. Lincoln appeared in such good spirits that someone pointed out, "I never saw Mr. Lincoln so cheerful and happy."[1] Once the meeting ended, Lincoln worked in his office and met his wife later for a carriage ride. She said to him, "Dear husband, you almost startle me by your great cheerfulness."[2]

Lincoln answered that he looked forward to the peaceful days ahead. He said, "We must both be more cheerful in the future; between the war and the loss of our darling Willie, we have both been very miserable."[3] Lincoln wanted to travel, to see the Pacific Ocean. And he thought about practicing law again in Illinois. Mary Todd Lincoln later recalled, "I never saw him so supremely cheerful—his manner was even playful."[4]

After the ride, the Lincolns returned to the White House for dinner. They planned to attend Ford's Theatre that evening, but Mary Todd Lincoln had a headache and didn't want to go. Lincoln reminded her that people expected them there, so she relented and accompanied him.

ABRAHAM LINCOLN and JOHN WILKES BOOTH

This image captures Lincoln's speech to a crowd of people at the White House on April 13, 1865. It would be his last.

THE ASSASSINATION

A Series of Unfortunate Events

Booth awakened on April 14 feeling depressed. His beloved Confederacy was dead. He had breakfast and then went to Ford's Theatre to pick up his mail. Many Washington actors had mail sent to Ford's. When he arrived, Booth learned that the Lincolns were expected to see the play *Our American Cousin*. Booth was elated. He knew Ford's well, having acted there many times, and he knew the play too. Booth could not believe his luck. The president was coming to him. He had eight hours to bring down the Union.

Booth called on Lewis Powell and George Atzerodt for help. He wanted Atzerodt to kill Vice President Andrew Johnson. Powell would target Secretary of State William Seward. Booth would kill Lincoln and General Grant, scheduled to attend the theater with the Lincolns. By killing this group, Booth hoped to destabilize the government, giving the Confederate government a chance to continue the war.

Before his theater outing, Lincoln stopped at the War Department to see if there was any news. His bodyguard, William Crook, urged Lincoln not to go to the theater. But Lincoln insisted on going, so Crook offered to escort him, serving as an extra bodyguard. The president turned him down, assuring him a guard would be there.

Booth had just eight hours to prepare to kill Lincoln and destroy the Union.

The Lincolns attended the play with Major Rathbone and his fiancée, Clara Harris. They arrived at Ford's at 8:30 p.m., half an hour late. (The Grants didn't make it.) They went up to the balcony to the presidential box, separate from the rest of the audience. They tried to enter quietly so as to not disturb the play,

ABRAHAM LINCOLN and JOHN WILKES BOOTH

but everyone noticed the president. The actors stopped and the orchestra played "Hail to the Chief." The audience jumped to their feet, clapping and cheering. Lincoln acknowledged them with a little bow and sat in a rocking chair the theater provided for him. The play resumed.

Booth entered Ford's at 9 p.m. He found out the scene in the play and then left. He returned with a rented horse. Booth asked Edwin Spangler, a theater employee, to hold the horse. Spangler objected, saying he was too busy, so another employee nicknamed John Peanut, held the horse instead. Booth left the theater and went to the Star Saloon, drinking whiskey.

Around 10 p.m., Booth left the saloon and went back to Ford's. The doorman recognized Booth and let him in. Booth arrived in time for a particular scene in the third act. He climbed the stairs to the balcony. He walked down the aisle to Lincoln's box, finding the police guard who should have been there missing. The guard had left to have a drink. Booth opened the door and entered a small outer room that led to the box where Lincoln sat. Earlier in the day, Booth had hidden a piece of wood that had been part of a music stand. He wedged it between the wall and the door so that no one outside could open the door.

Booth looked through the peephole at the president's box. The Lincolns were holding hands and enjoying the play. Todd Lincoln teasingly asked her husband, "What will Miss Harris think of my hanging on to you so?"[5] Lincoln responded, "She won't think anything about it."[6] These were his last words.

Booth had two weapons: his Derringer and a knife. He waited for a moment in the play that he knew would make the audience laugh. At 10:13, Booth opened the door and stepped into the box. The line from the play was delivered, and the audience, including the Lincolns, laughed. Booth shot Lincoln. The bullet lodged behind his right eye. Lincoln's head dropped and his body sagged in the chair. He never knew what hit him.

THE ASSASSINATION

Booth dropped his gun and moved toward the rail of the box. The sound of a gunshot startled audience members. Some thought it was part of the play, and others did not hear it at all. Major Rathbone, a Union army veteran, knew the sound of gunfire. He stepped in the direction of Lincoln and saw Booth. Rathbone grabbed Booth by the coat. Booth raised his knife to Rathbone intending to kill him, but Rathbone raised his arm to protect himself. Booth plunged his knife into Rathbone's arm. As blood flowed from his wound, Rathbone still pursued Booth, who had moved to the edge of the box to leap out of it onto the stage.

As Booth jumped, Rathbone grabbed his coattail causing Booth to lose his balance. On his way to the stage, Booth's boot spur caught on the flags that were decorating the box. Booth freed himself and landed on the stage off-balance. Some historians say that Booth broke a small bone above his left ankle when he landed. Others say the broken bone Booth had when captured stemmed from a horse falling on him during his escape.

Once on stage, Booth walked to the center, raised his bloody knife, and delivered his last performance. He cried out, "Sic semper tyrannis!"[7] The state motto of Virginia, the words meant "thus always to tyrants." Some say he also said, "The South is avenged!"[8]

Booth ran from the stage and made his way out of the theater, slashing his knife at anyone in his way. Rathbone shouted from the president's box, "Stop that man! Will no one stop that man?"[9] Clara Harris said loudly, "He has shot the president."[10] Mary Todd Lincoln sobbed.

Booth rushed out of the back of the theater. He jumped on his horse and galloped into the night. He wondered how the rest of his plan had gone. Were Seward and Johnson also dead? Booth would learn later that he was the only conspirator to execute his mission. Atzerodt lost his nerve and sat drinking all night.

ABRAHAM LINCOLN and JOHN WILKES BOOTH

This artist's painting of Lincoln's assassination captures how unguarded Lincoln was at Ford's Theatre, making it easy for Booth to attack and kill him.

THE ASSASSINATION

ABRAHAM LINCOLN and JOHN WILKES BOOTH

Powell went to Seward's house and found his target bedridden and recovering from a carriage accident. Powell stabbed Seward, injuring him gravely, but did not kill him.

Army surgeon Dr. Charles Leale sat in the audience at Ford's that night. He rushed to Lincoln's box to see if he could help. Leale observed that Lincoln's head was matted with blood. He found the bullet hole and said, "His wound is mortal; it is impossible for him to recover."[11]

Mary Todd Lincoln (1818–1882)

Although not elected directly, the First Lady has governmental responsibilities to fulfill. Mary Todd Lincoln served in this role during one of the most difficult times in the nation's history. Initially well received, she later alienated politicians, Washington society, and the press. Referred to as "the hellcat" by John Hay, Mary Todd Lincoln was a controversial First Lady. Historians have wondered whether she was mentally ill. If so, how did the deaths of three children, the Civil War, and her husband's murder affect her mental health?

Medical records don't provide a particular diagnosis, but we do know that Mary Todd Lincoln was a well-educated, intellectual, outgoing, and charming young woman. Over time, she developed many maladies: constant headaches, irritability, melancholy, pallor, fatigue, physical weakness, heart palpitations, mouth sores, swelling, and vision problems. According to Dr. John G. Sotos, a physician and scholar, she most likely suffered from pernicious anemia (PA), caused by a vitamin B12 deficiency.

PA was a fatal illness in Mary Todd Lincoln's era because physicians did not know its cause. It is easily treated today. Sotos hopes his theory will make people consider Mary Todd Lincoln with compassion rather than judgment.

THE ASSASSINATION

After shooting Lincoln, Booth jumped to the stage, made his way out of the theater, and jumped on a waiting horse to make his escape.

Leale did not want the president to die on a theater floor, but he also thought a bumpy ride to the White House would kill the president immediately. So Dr. Leale and the others moved Lincoln across the street to a boarding house and placed his body on a bed. Lincoln was so tall they positioned him diagonally, with his feet still hanging over the end. Todd Lincoln sat with him crying. Nothing more could be done. Abraham Lincoln drew his last breath April 15, 1865, at 7:22 a.m. Secretary of War Edwin Stanton looked at him and said, "Now he belongs to the ages."[12]

Lincoln's body was taken to the White House where thousands of people came to see it lying in state. Booth fled, trying to make it to Virginia where he believed he would receive a hero's welcome.

Chapter 8

LINCOLN'S AND BOOTH'S LEGACIES

Booth galloped away from Washington as fast as his horse could take him. Arriving at the Navy Yard Bridge at 11 p.m., three Union soldiers stopped him. They were guarding the spot where Booth hoped to cross the Potomac River's eastern branch. Aware that the news about Lincoln would not have reached the guards, Booth gave them his name and explained that he was heading to Maryland. The guards let him through. Davey Herold crossed the bridge a little while later, giving the guards a false name.

An Unexpected Ending

Booth and Herold went to Surratt's Tavern in Surrattsville, Maryland, to pick up weapons and binoculars he'd stored there. Booth boasted to the tavern keeper, "I am pretty certain that we have assassinated the president …"[1] Booth planned to reach Richmond, but his leg injury complicated his escape plan. He needed care from a doctor, so Booth went to the home of Dr. Samuel Mudd, a physician he knew from his earlier plan to kidnap Lincoln. Mudd examined Booth and diagnosed a break in the fibula, about two inches above the ankle joint. Mudd

LINCOLN'S AND BOOTH'S LEGACIES

Dr. Samuel Mudd provided medical care for Booth and let both Booth and Herold stay in his home. Mudd was eventually arrested and imprisoned for his actions.

splinted Booth's leg and, unaware of Lincoln's assassination, invited Booth and Herold to spend the night.

The next morning, April 15, Mudd went to town to buy supplies and visit with neighbors. Herold accompanied him. To Mudd's horror, he learned that Lincoln was dead, and Booth was the assassin. Telegrams had been sent all over the country to share the terrible news. Mudd kept quiet; he did not reveal that Booth was hiding in his farmhouse. Herold heard the news too and hurried back to the farm ahead of Mudd to warn Booth. Too injured to travel quickly, Booth waited at the farm hoping that Mudd had not given him up.

A furious Mudd returned home. He told Booth that while he offered previously to help kidnap Lincoln, he had never agreed to assist with murder. Now Booth had made him an accomplice to the assassination of the president! Mudd told Booth he had to leave but gave Booth the names of two confederates who could help him and Herold escape into Southern territory.

Booth and Herold next stopped at the house of Captain Samuel Cox, who decided to let them stay on his property. Cox told Booth and Herold that it was too dangerous for them to stay in his house but allowed them to hide in a wooded thicket of pine nearby. Cox also connected them with Thomas Jones, a boatman who would help them cross the Potomac into Virginia.

Jones, a Confederate Secret Service veteran, knew the Potomac well. He met Booth and Herold and told them to be patient, as they would have to wait for the right conditions to cross the river. Meanwhile, they had to stay hidden. Jones said he would bring them food. Booth asked for newspapers to read what people were saying about the assassination.

From April 17 to April 20, Booth and Herold hid in the pine thicket. Jones brought food and newspapers. Booth was horrified upon learning that both Northerners and Southerners had condemned him. Moreover, the nation viewed Lincoln as a

LINCOLN'S AND BOOTH'S LEGACIES

martyred hero. Even Lincoln's former political enemies praised him. Before Lincoln was shot, Northerners had been rejoicing the war's end. His death plunged them into a deep grief. People called Booth a vicious murderer.

No American president before Lincoln had ever been physically attacked, much less killed. In 1864, Secretary Seward had said, "Assassination is not an American practice or habit. And one so vicious and desperate cannot be engrafted into our political system."[2]

On April 20, Jones told Booth and Herold that conditions were ideal to cross the river. He put them in a boat and gave them the name of someone who would help them on the other side. Unfortunately for Booth and Herold, soldiers were patrolling the river, so the pair traveled farther north. They landed on the wrong shore but in a location Herold knew and where he had a friend to help them. A despondent Booth wrote in his diary, "After being hunted like a dog through swamps, woods, and last night being chased by gunboats till I was forced to return wet, cold and starving … I am here in despair. And why? For doing what Brutus was honored for … And yet I for striking down a tyrant … am looked upon as a common cutthroat."[3]

Booth and Herold got back on the boat on April 22. This time they made it to Virginia, landing on April 23. Several Confederate supporters met them, including Thomas Harbin, who took them to William Bryant. Bryant gave them horses and food and brought them to Dr. Richard Stewart, who fed them but who would not treat Booth's injury for fear of trouble

Booth was shocked to learn that his assassination of Lincoln was widely condemned and that Lincoln was elevated to hero status.

with the Union soldiers. Stewart refused to let Booth and Herold stay in his home and sent them to sleep in a tenant farmer's cabin.

Stewart's "want of hospitality"[4] incensed Booth. So, the actor-assassin and his partner next hired Charley, the tenant farmer's son, to take them to the village of Port Conway where they planned to cross the Rappahannock River. Booth and Herold took the ferry across. They met three Confederate soldiers who promised to help them when they reached the other side of the river. It was April 24.

Booth's Capture

Booth and Herold got off the ferry when it landed, and the soldiers headed toward Bowling Green, Virginia. One of the soldiers, Willie Jett, left the group and brought Booth and Herold to the farm of a man he knew, Richard Garrett. Booth introduced himself as James Boyd and said he was a wounded Confederate soldier making his way home. Garrett took in Booth and Herold, fed them a good supper, and told the men they could sleep in his house.

Booth slept in a bed that night, the first time in quite a few days. As Booth and Herold rested, the Union soldiers, in hot pursuit, were nearing. They arrived in Port Conway on April 25 and learned that men fitting the description of Booth and Herold had been seen heading toward Bowling Green. Meanwhile, Garrett was becoming suspicious of Booth and Herold and told them they could sleep in the tobacco barn that night but would have to leave in the morning. Garrett feared that Booth and Herold would steal his horses and leave in the night, so he had his son, Jack, padlock the barn door with Booth and Herold inside.

The Union soldiers barged into the Garrett farm at about 2 a.m. on April 26. Jack Garrett told them Booth and Herold were in the barn. The soldiers surrounded the barn and sent Jack

LINCOLN'S AND BOOTH'S LEGACIES

to get them. Booth refused to surrender. Herold gave himself up thinking they would let him go since he hadn't killed Lincoln. The soldiers told Booth to come out, but he offered to fight each man one at a time. His offer refused, Booth called out, "Well, my boys, you can prepare a stretcher for me then."[5] The soldiers set the barn ablaze.

Booth was visible through gaps in the barn walls. One of the soldiers, Boston Corbett, saw Booth in the light of the flames. Booth had a gun in one hand and a carbine in the other as he leaned on his crutch. Corbett shot Booth in the neck. The bullet severed Booth's spinal cord, paralyzing him.

Booth was carried from the barn and placed on a straw mattress on the porch. He whispered in a soft voice, "Tell ... Mother ... I died ... for my country."[6] Booth also begged the soldiers, "Kill me, kill me!"[7] Near the end, Booth asked one of the soldiers to lift his paralyzed hands so he could see them. Booth stared at them and softly said, "Useless, useless."[8] He then died. Per custom, the soldiers wrapped his body in an army blanket, so it could be carried back to Washington. Once it arrived, Secretary Stanton ordered an autopsy to verify the corpse's identity. Booth's body was buried in a crate in an unmarked grave at the Old Arsenal Penitentiary.

The Assassination's Aftermath

After learning Lincoln had been shot and Secretary Seward attacked, Secretary Stanton sent military guards to the homes of the vice president and every cabinet member. Stanton feared that a plot was underway to destabilize the US government so that the Confederacy could rise again. He worried that a Confederate army might be on its way to Washington, so he telegraphed General Grant requesting his return to the capital immediately. Stanton also initiated the manhunt for Booth and

ABRAHAM LINCOLN and JOHN WILKES BOOTH

LINCOLN'S AND BOOTH'S LEGACIES

Trapped in a burning barn and leaning on his crutch with weapons in his hands, Booth was an easy target for the soldier Boston Corbett, who shot him in the neck.

ABRAHAM LINCOLN and JOHN WILKES BOOTH

What Happened to Booth's Coconspirators?

Secretary Edwin Stanton hunted down everyone who plotted to kill Lincoln or helped Booth escape. The manhunt succeeded. Here are the fates of Booth's accomplices:

- Davey Herold: helped Booth escape; executed by hanging July 1865.
- George Atzerodt: part of the assassination plot; executed by hanging July 1865.
- Lewis Powell: part of the assassination plot; attacked Seward; executed by hanging July 1865.
- Mary Surratt: helped with the assassination plot; executed by hanging July 1865; first woman executed in America.
- Samuel Mudd: part of the kidnapping plot; helped Booth escape; sentenced to life in prison; pardoned in 1869 in recognition of his service in prison during an outbreak of yellow fever.
- Edwin Spangler: held Booth's horse briefly; sentenced to six years in prison; pardoned in 1869.
- John Surratt: escaped to Europe; captured in Egypt in 1867; tried in 1868; not convicted.
- Samuel Arnold: part of the kidnapping plot; sentenced to life in prison; pardoned in 1869.
- Michael O'Laughlen: part of the kidnapping plot; sentenced to life in prison; died of yellow fever in 1867.

LINCOLN'S AND BOOTH'S LEGACIES

his coconspirators: Powell, Surratt, Herold, and Atzerodt. Surratt was then in New York, nowhere near the assassination. He knew he would be arrested anyway, so he fled to Canada. He went to Italy and joined the Pope's army, serving as a soldier for a year.

Booth's actions devastated his family. Asia was five months pregnant when she saw the front page of the newspaper reporting that her brother had killed the president. June Booth was performing in Cincinnati, Ohio, and woke up on April 15 intending to take a morning walk. The hotel desk clerk warned him not to go out. June returned to his room shortly before an angry mob stormed the lobby looking for him. June hid in his room until the staff smuggled him out on April 17. June planned to stay with Asia in Philadelphia until things became calmer.

Booth's mother and sister Rosalie were living in New York City with Edwin when they heard that Booth killed Lincoln. Booth's mother hoped her son would shoot himself rather than go through the spectacle of a trial. Edwin was acting in Boston when he heard. The remainder of his Boston season was canceled, and he went home to New York to be with his mother and sister.

Once June got to Philadelphia, he was arrested. Asia's husband, John Sleeper Clarke, was also arrested. Both men were imprisoned—Clarke for more than a month and June for almost two months. Asia was kept under house arrest; being pregnant kept her out of jail. Edwin was essentially under house arrest in New York. He received lots of hate mail, and his acting future seemed uncertain. Booth's family hadn't done anything wrong or known of his plans. Still, the authorities treated them like criminals.

About seven months after the assassination, Edwin asked Secretary Stanton if he could have his brother's remains. Edwin explained that his mother wanted to see her son properly buried. Stanton said he could not just yet because public emotion was

ABRAHAM LINCOLN and JOHN WILKES BOOTH

Another Lincoln and Booth Connection

On vacation from college, Robert Todd Lincoln was traveling from New York City to Washington, DC. The train stopped in Jersey City and Robert got off and stepped on to the crowded platform. It was so crowded his back pressed against the train. Suddenly, the train moved, and Robert fell into the space between the train cars and off the platform. Fortunately, a hand reached out and grabbed Robert's coat collar, yanking him back up onto the platform. Robert turned to thank his rescuer and saw that it was none other than Edwin Booth, the brother of John Wilkes Booth. Robert recognized Edwin, a famous actor, but Edwin did not recognize him. Edwin later learned that he had saved Lincoln's son. This brought Edwin a small measure of comfort in the assassination's aftermath.

---

too high. Edwin returned to the stage in January 1866, about nine months after the assassination. Some people were happy to see him, and others were outraged. Edwin also reimbursed Richard Garrett for his lost barn.

In 1867, Edwin tried once more to get his brother's body. He was unsuccessful. Two years later, Edwin was permitted to retrieve his brother's remains as long as he stayed quiet about it. Edwin had the body brought to Baltimore, where it was buried in the Booth family plot in the Greenmount Cemetery in an unmarked grave.

Asia and her husband moved to England and never returned to the United States. Asia's husband demanded a divorce. He wanted nothing more to do with the Booth family. They did not divorce, but their marriage was irrevocably damaged.

LINCOLN'S AND BOOTH'S LEGACIES

In the final analysis, what is Booth's legacy? He succeeded in killing Lincoln but failed in every other way. He did not topple the government or inspire the South to fight to victory. He did not undo the Emancipation Proclamation. Instead, he made Northerners so angry that they were more vengeful after the war than Lincoln ever intended. And he caused both his and Lincoln's families deep pain.

After Lincoln's body was taken to the White House, his widow shut herself into a guest room. Inconsolable, she would talk only to Tad. Thousands came to pay their respects to Lincoln; the line of people stretched a mile. The funeral took place in the White House's East Room, but Mary Todd Lincoln didn't attend.

Lincoln's funeral procession traveled by train from Washington, DC, to Springfield, Illinois. This photo shows Lincoln's coffin being pulled along a street during a stop along the way.

ABRAHAM LINCOLN and JOHN WILKES BOOTH

Lincoln's image is carved into Mt. Rushmore along with three other highly regarded presidents: George Washington, Thomas Jefferson, and Theodore Roosevelt.

LINCOLN'S AND BOOTH'S LEGACIES

Afterward, Lincoln's coffin was carried to the Capitol building where four thousand black citizens paid their respects.

On April 21, Lincoln's body was placed on a train, along with son Willie's body, back to Illinois. During the trip, eleven more ceremonies in various cities took place. More than eighty-five thousand people turned out in New York City alone. The train arrived in Springfield on May 3. Lincoln and Willie were buried in the Oak Ridge Cemetery the next day.

Lincoln died a hero. Since then, his stature has only grown. In 1909, the hundredth anniversary of Lincoln's birth, Confederate veterans speculated that had Lincoln lived, the period after the war wouldn't have been so hard. Such veterans were angry with Booth for so upsetting the North that the South felt its vengeance rather than the peaceful reconciliation Lincoln had promised. Union veterans viewed Booth as murderer of the man who fought to preserve America.

Scholars consider Lincoln one of the best US presidents. In 1922, the Lincoln Memorial was dedicated in Washington, DC. The number of memorials bearing his name is too long to tally. The slain president's face not only appears on US currency but on Mt. Rushmore as well. Because Lincoln is former president Barack

Obama's favorite president, Obama used Lincoln's Bible during his swearing-in ceremonies in 2008 and 2012.

Both Abraham Lincoln and John Wilkes Booth live on in memory. Lincoln is remembered for saving the Union and ending slavery. In doing so, he was the first president to address the nation's "original sin."[9] And Booth was a tragic figure, linked forever to a man he never knew but hated so deeply it became an obsession.

CHRONOLOGY

ABRAHAM LINCOLN

1809
Abraham Lincoln is born in Kentucky.

1812
Thomas Lincoln Jr. is born. He dies in infancy.

1818
Lincoln's mother, Nancy Hanks Lincoln, dies of milk sickness.

1819
Thomas Lincoln Sr. marries Sarah Bush Johnston.

1828
Lincoln's sister, Sarah, dies giving birth.

Lincoln and Allen Gentry pilot a flatboat to New Orleans. Lincoln sees a slave auction.

1831
Lincoln goes to New Orleans by flatboat. Upon returning, he settles in New Salem, Illinois.

1832
Lincoln runs for the Illinois Assembly. He loses the election. The Black Hawk War breaks out, and Lincoln joins the Illinois militia.

ABRAHAM LINCOLN and JOHN WILKES BOOTH

1833
Lincoln becomes postmaster of New Salem and a deputy county surveyor.

1834
Lincoln is elected to the Illinois General Assembly. He is reelected in 1836, 1838, and 1840.

1836
Lincoln receives his license to practice law.

1839
Lincoln meets Mary Todd. They become engaged the following year.

1841
Lincoln breaks off his engagement with Mary Todd. They reunite after a year and marry in 1842.

1843
Lincoln's first son, Robert Todd Lincoln, is born.

1846
Lincoln is elected to the United States Congress. His second son, Edward (Eddie) Baker Lincoln is born.

1850
Eddie Lincoln dies. He was not quite four years old. William (Willie) Wallace Lincoln is born ten months later.

1853
Thomas (Tad) Lincoln is born.

CHRONOLOGY

1855
Lincoln runs for the United States Senate. He loses the election.

1858
Lincoln runs for the Senate as a Republican. He debates the Democratic nominee, Stephen Douglas, seven times. Lincoln loses the election.

1860
Lincoln is nominated a presidential candidate at the Republican National Convention. Lincoln is elected sixteenth president of the United States. The secession of Southern states begins with South Carolina.

1861
More states secede. Lincoln is inaugurated. The Civil War commences.

1862
Willie Lincoln dies.

1863
Lincoln issues the Emancipation Proclamation. The Civil War takes a turn in favor of the Union with the defeats of Confederate forces in Gettysburg and Vicksburg. Lincoln delivers the Gettysburg Address.

1864
Lincoln puts General Ulysses Grant in charge of the entire Union army. Lincoln is reelected to a second term.

1865

The Thirteenth Amendment to the Constitution passes. It abolishes slavery.

Lincoln is inaugurated.

General Lee surrenders.

John Wilkes Booth shoots Lincoln in the head.

Lincoln dies.

Lincoln's funeral is held.

Lincoln is laid to rest.

JOHN WILKES BOOTH

1838

John Wilkes Booth is born in Maryland.

1845

The Booth family begins a pattern of living part of the year in Baltimore and part on their farm.

1846

Adelaide Booth, the first wife of Booth's father, shows up in Maryland and informs the family that they never divorced.

1851

Booth's father divorces Adelaide. Booth's father marries John's mother.

1852

Booth's father dies.

CHRONOLOGY

1857
Booth is hired by the Arch Theatre in Philadelphia, Pennsylvania.

1858
Booth is hired by the Marshall Theatre in Richmond, Virginia.

1859
Booth enlists in the Virginia militia and joins a contingent of men guarding the abolitionist, John Brown. Booth witnesses John Brown's execution.

1860
Booth is hired by Canning's Dramatic Company. He goes on tour as a star actor.

1863
Booth performs in *The Marble Heart* at Ford's Theatre in Washington, DC. Lincoln attends a performance.

1864
Booth plans to kidnap Lincoln. He attends Lincoln's second inauguration.

1865
Booth and his coconspirators attempt to kidnap Lincoln. They are unsuccessful.

Booth hears Lincoln declare his support for having voting rights granted to African Americans.

ABRAHAM LINCOLN and JOHN WILKES BOOTH

Booth and his coconspirators make plans to kill President Lincoln, Vice President Johnson, Secretary Seward, and General Grant.

Booth shoots Lincoln in the head.

Booth is captured and shot in the neck. He dies from his wound.

1869
Booth's remains are released to his family and buried in the family's cemetery plot, in an unmarked grave.

CHAPTER NOTES

INTRODUCTION
1. David Herbert Donald, *Lincoln* (New York, NY: Simon & Schuster, 1995), p. 567.
2. James Cross Giblin, *Good Brother Bad Brother* (New York, NY: Clarion Books, 2005), p. 114.
3. Ibid.
4. Ibid.

CHAPTER 1
Lincoln's Boyhood
1. David Herbert Donald, *Lincoln* (New York, NY: Simon & Schuster, 1995), p. 19.
2. Ibid., pp. 23–24.
3. Ibid., p. 30.
4. Ibid., p. 33.

CHAPTER 2
Booth's Early Years
1. Terry Alford, *Fortune's Fool: The Life of John Wilkes Booth* (New York, NY: Oxford University Press, 2015), p. 26.
2. "Abraham Lincoln's Assassination," Rogernorton.com, accessed December 8, 2017, http://rogerjnorton.com/Lincoln72.html.
3. Alford, p. 11.
4. Ibid., p. 17.
5. Ibid., p. 18.
6. Ibid., p. 19.
7. Ibid., p. 20.
8. Ibid., p. 22.

CHAPTER 3
New Salem and the Presidency
1. David Herbert Donald, *Lincoln* (New York, NY: Simon & Schuster, 1995), p. 44.

2. Ibid., p. 45.
3. Ibid., p. 55.
4. Ibid., p. 66.
5. Ibid.
6. Tanya Lee Stone, *Abraham Lincoln* (New York, NY: DK Publishing, 2005), p. 31.
7. Donald, p. 206.

CHAPTER 4
Politics and Acting

1. James Cross Giblin, *Good Brother Bad Brother* (New York, NY: Clarion Books, 2005), p. 51.
2. Terry Alford, *Fortune's Fool: The Life of John Wilkes Booth* (New York, NY: Oxford University Press, 2015), p. 43.
3. Ibid.
4. Ibid.
5. Giblin, p. 53.
6. Ibid.
7. Ibid.
8. Alford, p. 68.
9. Giblin, p. 57.
10. Alford, p. 97.

CHAPTER 5
The Presidential Election

1. "Abraham Lincoln First Inaugural Address," Bartleby.com, accessed December 8, 2017, http://www.bartleby.com/124/pres31.html.
2. Terry Alford, *Fortune's Fool: The Life of John Wilkes Booth* (New York, NY: Oxford University Press, 2015), p. 106.
3. Ibid.

CHAPTER NOTES

CHAPTER 6
The Civil War

1. Tanya Lee Stone, *Abraham Lincoln* (New York, NY: DK Publishing, 2005), p. 69.
2. Ibid., p. 73.
3. Ibid., p. 79.
4. David Herbert Donald, *Lincoln* (New York, NY: Simon & Schuster, 1995), p. 405.
5. Ibid., p. 431.
6. Ibid., p. 464.
7. Stone, p. 101.
8. Ibid., p. 103.
9. "Abraham Lincoln Second Inaugural Address," Bartleby.com, accessed December 8, 2017, http://www.bartleby.com/124/pres32.html.
10. James Cross Giblin, *Good Brother Bad Brother* (New York, NY: Clarion Books, 2005), 82.
11. Ibid.
12. Ibid.

CHAPTER 7
The Assassination

1. Tanya Lee Stone, *Abraham Lincoln* (New York, NY: DK Publishing, 2005), p. 113.
2. James L. Swanson, *Chasing Lincoln's Killer* (New York, NY: Scholastic Press, 2009), p. 29.
3. Stone, p. 113.
4. Swanson, p. 30.
5. Stone, p. 114.
6. Ibid.
7. Swanson, p. 43.
8. Ibid.
9. Ibid., p. 45.
10. Ibid., p. 45.
11. Ibid., p. 69.

12. David Herbert Donald, *Lincoln* (New York, NY: Simon & Schuster, 1995), p. 599.

CHAPTER 8
Lincoln's and Booth's Legacies

1. James L. Swanson, *Chasing Lincoln's Killer* (New York, NY: Scholastic Press, 2009), p. 84.
2. James Cross Giblin, *Good Brother Bad Brother* (New York, NY: Clarion Books, 2005), p. 132.
3. Ibid., p. 140.
4. Ibid., p. 141.
5. Ibid., p. 147.
6. Ibid., p. 148.
7. Ibid.
8. Ibid.
9. Roger Cohen, "Beyond America's Original Sin," NYTimes.com, March 20, 2008, http://www.nytimes.com/2008/03/20/opinion/20cohen.html.

GLOSSARY

abolition Movement to set slaves free and end the practice of slavery.

Confederate/Confederacy The group of states that left the United States to form their own country.

Democratic Party In the nineteenth century, a political organization that tolerated or supported slavery.

Electoral College The actual group that elects the president of the United States. The popular vote in a state directs the electors how to vote.

elocution The skill of clear speech and pronunciation.

majority In voting, a number that is greater than half of the total.

plantation A large-scale farm that cultivates cash crops such as cotton, tobacco, and sugar.

plurality In voting, a number that is greater than others but not more than half.

Republican Party In the nineteenth century, a political organization that was against the spread of slavery and for the abolition of slavery.

secede/secession The act of a state leaving the United States.

survey To record, evaluate and describe the areas and features of a land area to produce maps.

surveyor A person who surveys professionally.

tariff A tax to be paid for imports and/or exports.

telegraph A message sent along a wire by transmitting electrical signals.

Union The United States of America.

Whig Party A nineteenth-century political organization that supported protective tariffs, national banking, and government funding for infrastructure improvements.

FURTHER READING

BOOKS

Anderson, Marilyn. *Abraham Lincoln: Pivotal Presidents, Profiles in Leadership*. New York, NY: Rosen, 2013.

Cumming, Judy Dodge. *The Civil War: The Struggle That Divided America* (Inquire and Investigate). White River Junction, VT: Nomad Press, Reprint Edition, 2017.

Helweg, Laura. *How Abraham Lincoln Fought the Civil War*. New York, NY: Enslow Publishing, 2017.

Landau, Elaine. *Lincoln's Emancipation Proclamation: Would You Sign the Great Document?* New York, NY: Enslow Publishing, 2015.

WEBSITES

Abraham Lincoln
www.history.com/topics/us-presidents/abraham-lincoln
This is a succinct biography of Lincoln.

Abraham Lincoln: Mini Biography
www.biography.com/people/abraham-lincoln-9382540
Biographical sketch of Lincoln.

John Wilkes Booth
www.history.com/american-civil-war/john-wilkes-booth
Information about the life of John Wilkes Booth.

John Wilkes Booth: Execution of John Brown
www.biography.com/people/john-wilkes-booth-9219681
Highlights from John Wilkes Booth's life.

FILMS

Lincoln (2012)
Killing Lincoln (2013)

INDEX

A
abolitionists, 38, 44, 53, 76, 78
American Indians, 11
Arch Theatre, 31, 48–49, 51
Armstrong, Jack, 33

B
Baltimore, Maryland, 24, 25, 28–29, 31, 51, 66, 108
Black Hawk War, 33, 35, 36
black voting rights, 8, 83
Boone, Daniel, 10
Booth, Adelaide, 26
Booth, Asia, 22, 24, 25, 31, 52, 55, 84, 107, 108
Booth, Edwin, 24, 25, 28–29, 31, 48, 51–52, 57, 72, 83, 107–108
Booth, John Wilkes
   acting career, 22, 31, 48–49, 51–52, 55, 56, 83, 84
   ancestors, 22, 24
   assassination of Lincoln, 8, 22, 91–93
   birth, 24
   capture, 102–103
   childhood, 25–29
   death, 103
   education, 25, 27
   and Grays militia, 53, 55
   legacy, 109, 112
   manhunt for, 98, 100–102, 106
   plan to kidnap Lincoln, 84, 86, 88
   political opinions, 57, 72
   siblings, 22, 24, 25, 51
   support for the Confederacy, 83–84, 86, 91
Booth, Junius Brutus, 22, 24–28, 48
Booth, Mary Ann, 22, 24, 26–29
Booth, Richard, 25
Brown, John, 44, 53

C
Civil War, 7, 63, 69, 73–74, 76, 78–79, 81, 83–85, 96
Clarke, John Sleeper, 31, 49, 84, 107
Clary's Grove gang, 32–33
coconspirators of Lincoln assassination, 105–107
Confederacy
   formation of, 7
   surrender of, 8
Confederate Secret Service, 88, 100

D
Davis, Jefferson, 64, 69, 84

INDEX

Democratic Party, 44, 56, 58, 62, 81
Douglas, Stephen, 44, 45, 47, 56, 58, 62, 68
Douglass, Frederick, 76, 78
Dred Scott decision, 45

E

education, nineteenth-century, 27
Emancipation Proclamation, 78, 79, 81, 109

F

flatboats, 18, 20
Ford's Theater, 84, 89, 91–92, 96

G

Gettysburg Address, 79
Grant, Ulysses S., 74, 79, 81, 83, 89, 91, 103

H

habeas corpus, 73, 74, 86
Hay, John, 60, 64, 66, 96
Herndon, William, 42, 43, 66
Herold, Davey, 86, 98, 100–103, 106, 107

J

Jackson, Andrew, 24
Johnston, Sally Bush, 15, 17, 66

K

Kansas-Nebraska Act, 44

L

Lee, Robert E., 7, 79, 83, 88, 89
Lincoln, Abraham
  ancestors, 9–11
  assassination, 8, 91–93
  birth, 13
  childhood, 9–15, 17
  children, 41, 42, 43, 76, 89
  and the Civil War, 7, 64, 66, 73–74, 76, 78–79, 81, 83–84
  debates with Stephen Douglas, 47
  depression, 39
  education, 17, 32
  funeral and burial, 109, 111
  and the Illinois State Legislature, 33, 35–36, 37
  law career, 36–37, 41–42, 43, 66
  legacy, 109, 111–112
  military service, 33, 35
  presidential elections, 58–60, 62–64, 81
  presidential inaugurations, 68, 83, 85, 86
  presidential term, 64, 66
  as a river pilot, 18, 20–21
  siblings, 11, 13, 15, 17–18
  and slavery, 17, 37–38, 42, 56, 68, 76, 78, 81

speeches, 8, 47, 68, 83
as a US congressman, 42
wedding, 41
Lincoln, Mary Todd, 39, 41, 42, 66, 76, 89, 92, 93, 96, 109
Lincoln, Nancy Hanks, 11, 13–15
Lincoln, Robert Todd, 41, 43, 89, 108
Lincoln, Thomas (father), 10–11, 13–15, 18, 20, 41
Lincoln Memorial, 111

M

Marshall Theater, 51–52, 56
Milton Academy, 27–28
Missouri Compromise, 44, 45, 53
Mt. Rushmore, 111
Mudd, Samuel, 98, 100, 106

N

New Salem, Illinois, 21, 32–33, 35
Nicolay, John, 60, 64, 66

O

Obama, Barack, 111–112
Offutt, Denton, 20–21, 32–33
Owens, Mary, 39

P

Philadelphia, 31, 49, 66, 78, 84, 107

Powell, Lewis, 86, 91, 106, 107
presidential election of 1860, 58–60, 62–64
presidential election of 1864, 81

R

Republican Party, 9, 44, 47, 56, 58, 62, 81
Rutledge, Ann, 38–39
Rutledge, James, 32–33, 38

S

secession, 7, 56, 64, 69, 74
Seward, William, 91, 93, 96, 101, 103, 106
slaveholders, 38–39
slavery
  legislation, 44
  Lincoln's opposition to, 13, 37–38
Speed, Joshua, 36–39, 41
Springfield, Illinois, 41, 42, 60, 66, 111
Stanton, Edwin, 74, 97, 103, 106, 107
Stuart, John Todd, 36, 41

T

telegraphy, 63

W

Whig Party, 35–36, 42, 44